The Secret Diary

The Secret Diary

The True Story of World War II POW Marvin Doyle

Michelle Wright

CONTENTS

This book is dedicated to my mother, Gail Reaves Wright. Her love of learning, dedication to helping others and passion for life is the reason this story is being told.

Contributing photos and confirmation of prison camp details: 303rdBG.com, merkki.com, Down in Flames Ray Parker Mill City Press, Parachute to Berlin Lowell Bennett Casemate Publishers, and The National WWII Museum archives

Editor and cover and book design by Anthony Landolina

First Printing, 2024

THE STORY OF MARVIN DOYLE

If caught, his captors would have killed him but Marvin Doyle was determined to document the truth in case he didn't make it out alive. There was also another reason; Marvin thought the sooner he'd write down what happened the sooner he'd be able erase it from his tortured mind.

This is the true story of aerial gunner Sergeant Marvin Doyle, a World War II prisoner of war who kept a secret diary while held cap-

tive in Stalag Luft 1, a German prison camp by the Baltic Sea. Marvin was shot down on November 4, 1944 in a B-24 bomber over Mostar, Yugoslavia. He wanted history to know what he and his crew endured for America's freedom. Even more than that, he wanted the love of his life, his wife Anne, to know what happened to him. He had to be resourceful to make this happen.

Once he got to Stalag Luft 1, the Red Cross sent parcels to the POW camps in accordance with the Geneva Convention rules. Those care packages included food, soap and cigarettes. He began to collect the wrappers from the discarded cigarette packs, and he wrote his secret diary on the back of 37 of them. He wrote if it was discovered, he would be put in solitary confinement and only given bread and water but knew this had to be documented.

As you'll see in his diary, he detailed the terror of his plane being shot down, the hard parachute landing in which he was injured, his capture by dozens of Germans ready to shoot him on the spot, the overwhelming hunger and the unbearable cold. He wrote about the frigid temperature that tormented him as it reached 30 degrees below zero. He described the power being cut off and having to melt snow for water. He detailed being forced to walk miles through a blinding snowstorm to get from one prison camp to the next. He would later talk of his appreciation to his squadron for refusing to leave him behind for the Nazis to kill despite his struggle to keep up on the march because of his injuries. He shared how he was haunted by the tail gunner who froze with fear as their plane was going down and was too scared to pull his chute. He describes eating bugs and drinking vile coffee. And he writes of dreaming of sweet Anne and how he hoped she was waiting for him.

Additionally, he wrote inspirational poems about hope, courage and perseverance. His poem, "Courage", is especially inspiring as it encourages his fellow POWs "to climb that hill, boys..... remember you're Americans and when you reach the crest you'll see a valley cool and green, America at her best."

Perhaps surprisingly, he didn't write of his hatred for his captors despite the horrific conditions. Instead, he hoped for peace for both sides. He wrote, "I have been in the air and on the ground and I know how horrible war can be. It is terrible that so many people have to be slaughtered even though they are your enemies."

Especially poignant is his treasured letter from General George C. Marshall, Chief of Staff of the Army, in which he warns about the importance of avoiding war in the future. At the war's end, Marshall wrote to Marvin and his fellow servicemen, "Choose your leaders wisely — that is the way to keep ours the country for which you fought. Make sure that those leaders are determined to maintain peace throughout the world. You know what war is. You know that we must not have another. As individuals, you can prevent it if you give to the task which lies ahead the same spirit which you displayed in uniform."

My family lived next to Anne Doyle for more than thirty years, and my mother was her caretaker. Anne kept all of the things Marvin brought back from the war in pristine condition, including his secret diary. She gave them to my mother who gave them to me, and I am honored to compile Marvin's inspirational journey to bring to fruition his wish of ensuring history knows the real story of what happened as he sacrificed so much to keep America free.

Anne and Marvin Doyle

MARVIN'S SACRIFICE

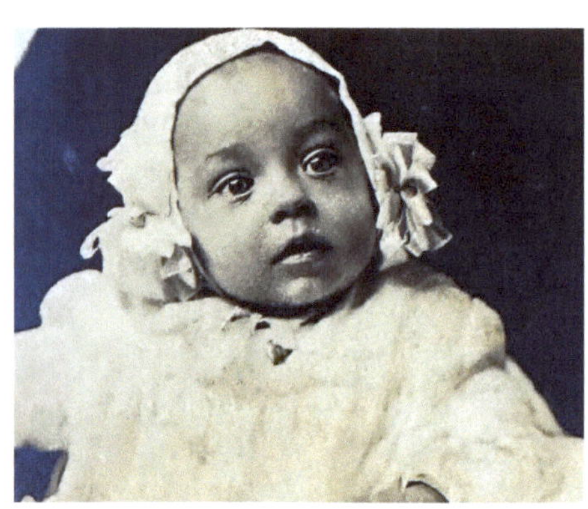

Marvin Doyle was born January 28, 1911. He was the only child of Walter and Adelaide Doyle. Though he was born in Oklahoma City, Oklahoma, the family moved to Roanoke, Virginia when Marvin was young.

As a child, he dreamed of owning his own business and after high school, that goal took him about an hour higher up into the mountains of Virginia to a small town called Blacksburg. He began studying business at Virginia Polytechnic Institute, known as Virginia Tech. The school's iconic limestone buildings were beautiful but Blacksburg sits on an elevated plateau between the Blue Ridge Mountains and Allegheny Mountains, and Marvin's freshman year was spent battling the winter. Christmas Day in Blacksburg in 1930 was negative six degrees.

But as spring arrived and daffodils started to bloom all over campus, his heart warmed when he met Anne Elizabeth Whitlow. She was two and a half years younger than Marvin and while she wasn't a college student, she worked in town for Chesapeake and Potomac Telephone Company. He asked Anne to the Cotillion Club's Spring Dance April 4th, 1930. He was smitten.

The Cotillion Club
of the
Virginia Polytechnic Institute
cordially invites you to attend the
Midwinter Dances
to be held in the War Memorial Gymnasium
Friday and Saturday, February thirteenth and fourteenth
nineteen hundred and thirty-one
Blacksburg, Virginia

Formal   W. H. Shewbridge, Secretary

The Cotillion Club
of the
Virginia Polytechnic Institute
cordially invites you to attend the
Spring Dances
to be held in the War Memorial Gymnasium
Friday and Saturday, April fourth and fifth
nineteen hundred and thirty
Blacksburg, Virginia

Formal   C. H. Lewis, Jr., Secretary

Anne was born in nearby Rocky Mount, Virginia. Her father farmed and was also a driller for Virginia Bridge and Iron Company. Her mother kept the house. Anne had one older sister, Marla, and a younger sister, Blanche. Anne was independent and at seventeen, she moved to Blacksburg to work for the telephone company. She loved getting dressed up for work every day; a far cry from her upbringing on the farm. It was rare in the 1930s for a woman to move away to pursue a career, and her parents and sisters weren't sure what to think of her. Marvin thought she was perfect.

They dated through that year and by the time he asked her to the Midwinter Dance on Valentine's Day of 1931, they were talking about spending their lives together. They were married later that same year on November 6 in Roanoke. He was twenty-one, and she was eighteen.

Marvin continued to earn his degree while they were married, and Anne continued working at the C&P Telephone Company. After graduation, they moved north to Arlington, Virginia. Anne transferred her job with the telephone company, and Marvin took a job with Life and Casualty Insurance Company in Washington, D.C. His mother would die a few years later at the young age of fifty. Her death changed Marvin's world. He didn't realize his world was about to change even more and crush the plans of so many Americans his age.

Germany invaded Poland in September 1939. The next year the United States Congress passed the Selective Service Act which required all men between the ages of twenty-one and thirty-five to register for military service. Marvin was twenty-nine when he registered in October of 1940.

Despite trying to avoid involvement in World War II, the United States was pulled into the conflict with the bombing of Pearl Harbor in December of 1941. Marvin checked his draft card numbers while listening to the first draft lottery on the radio on October 29th, 1940, as blindfolded Secretary of War Henry Stimson reached into a fishbowl and pulled out the first capsule containing draft numbers. From a nearby podium President Roosevelt announced the number drawn: 158. Across the country 6,175 young men held that number and were assigned to which branch of service they'd report. This was not Marvin's number. He would go back to work and wait for the next lottery draw.

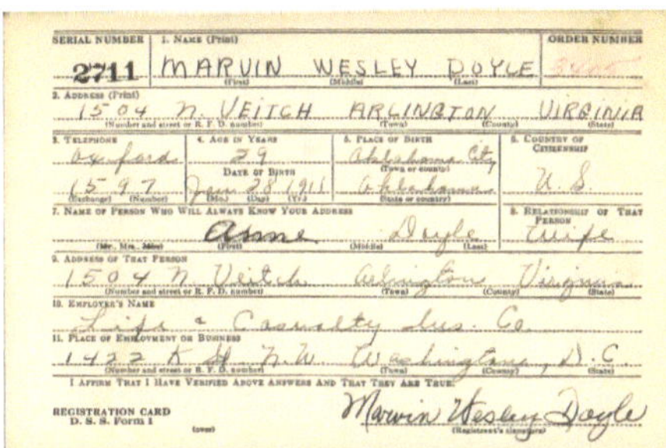

Marvin's draft card was finally pulled a year-and-a-half later, May 4, 1943. He was thirty-three and drafted into the Army's Air Force. Like so many other drafted young men, he had never stepped foot in an airplane before. Now, not only would he learn how it felt to fly, but he was about to learn how to fight a war 20,000 feet in the sky. He packed up and left for aerial gunner training across the country in Walla Walla, Washington while Anne stayed in Arlington, Virginia in their home at 1506 North Vetch Street. They were hoping for a quick end to the war so they could reunite.

Before long, his training took him to Miami Beach, Florida where he enjoyed the hot temperatures and sunny beaches. The Army moved him on to Scott Field, Illinois and then Harlingen Field, Texas. While he was going around the country training he

faithfully wrote Anne letters and eagerly waited to get letters from her. He'd address his letters to "Anne Darling." Mail ran slow and Marvin was frustrated as he waited to hear from her.

Marvin at training in Miami Beach

At thirty-three, he was older than most of the other servicemen and became a natural leader. He was in the 450th bomber group nicknamed "Cotton Tails" and assigned to the 720th squadron as a waist gunner. His squadron flew to an Allied base in Italy September 19, 1944 with no idea what lay ahead. It was the first time he'd ever been out of the country.

The skies were clear on the Monday morning he took off in a B-24 bomber. It was November 6, 1944 at 10:30 a.m. and his crew headed for a bombing raid in Yugoslavia. It was only their sixth mission. His journal detailed who was in his squadron and their position.

Front Row (left to right):
- Bombardier: George Maljanian from Providence, Rhode Island
- Co-Pilot Alvin Millspaugh from Oakland, California
- Pilot: Ireland R. Kearns from Parkersburg, West Virginia
- Navigator: James H. Mouth from Bastrop, Texas

Back Row (left to right):
- Radio Man: Robert J. McVay from Pittsburgh, PA
- Nose Gunner: Michael Pruvenock from Gary, Indiana
- Tail Gunner: Wayne Rinnie from Seaside, Oregon
- Aerial Gunner: Marvin Doyle from Alexandria, Virginia
- Ball Gunner: Rocco L. Stefano from Buffalo, New York

Not Pictured
- Engineer: Joseph Matusavich from Chicago, Illinois

The men in the squadron didn't have a lot in common. Each crew member came from a different state in America. From the farmlands to the coasts, from big cities to small towns, this unlikely group joined together on a single objective to take down Hitler's Third Reich.

Germany had invaded Yugoslavia three-and-a-half years earlier. It only took a few weeks for Yugoslavia to surrender to the Nazis. Marvin's squadron was told to avoid flying over Mostar because while there were only four batteries of anti-aircraft artillery guns, more commonly referred to as flak gunners, positioned there, they were known to be very accurate. The B-24 (#165) which they climbed into that morning had already been in more than 100 missions. Marvin was stationed on the left wing by the open window. He knew that would mean a frigid flight over the Adriatic Sea, so he put on his fifty-pound heated flight suit to keep him warm.

They didn't know it at the time, but they had drifted over Mostar and those four flak gunner batteries lived up to their accurate reputation. Marvin's plane was under attack. They started losing altitude and Marvin counted more than 100 holes in the plane. They attempted to "strip the ship" to lighten the load and dropped their bombs along with everything else they could dump out. It was no use. The co-pilot Alvin Millspaugh yelled that it was time "to get the hell out." One by one, the airmen secured their parachutes and jumped out. In the months of training the crew received before being deployed to the war, they were never trained how to jump from an airplane. Millspaugh later recalled they were only told to pull the ring to open their chute and hope for the best.

Marvin looked back for the young tail gunner Wayne "Rinnie" Rinne who was from Seaside, Oregon. He was lying in the catwalk frozen with fear. Marvin yanked him up, shoved him against the door, shook him and

Wayne Rinne and Marvin Doyle

made him understand they had to jump. Overcome with terror, Rinne refused. Then, suddenly, he calmly smiled at Marvin and jumped. Marvin would later learn Rinnie never pulled his parachute and fell to his death.

Marvin ran back for a pack of cigarettes and then jumped himself. He described pulling his chute and letting the wind carry him toward a river where he managed to land on some rocks on the riverbank. He hit hard and severely sprained his left ankle and then fought to get his chute off so it wouldn't drag him into the river. His fight to survive suddenly stopped when seconds later what seemed like a hundred German soldiers surrounded him. The Germans took his .45 caliber pistol, wallet, pen, helmet, scarf, and cigarettes. Marvin raised his hands and waited to be shot. Seeing his wristwatch, they took it, too. It was 1:10 p.m.

The Nazis made him stand up, but he couldn't put pressure on his left foot. As they forced him to a house about a hundred yards away, he could barely hobble. Seeing he was injured, they took off his boot, looked at his bruised, swollen ankle and laughed. They threw his boot back at him and gestured for him to put it back on saying, "Americans like to die with their boots on." Thankfully, at that moment a German officer rode up on a motorcycle and saved Marvin's life by determining he would be a prisoner of war.

From Mostar, he was moved to several additional prison camps: Sarajevo, Brod, Vienna, Frankfort and onto Wetzlar. Along the way there was constant Allied bombing raids all around him, and he could only hope the Allies were accurate and he wouldn't be killed by friendly fire. As the Nazis kept moving the POWs, Marvin described having to walk for miles in a blinding snowstorm. He would also later tell his wife that during those marches his ankle was still injured so badly that the Germans threatened to shoot him because he was slowing down the march. His squadron refused to let that happen and took turns carrying him as needed. This meant an incredible amount to Marvin, and he thought about the sacrifice his men made on his behalf for the rest of his life. On December 23rd, they arrived at Stalag Luft 1 in Barth, Germany where he'd stay for the remainder of his capture.

Back home, Anne received a Western Union telegram on November 17th, eleven days after Marvin's plane was shot down. It only said, "The secretary of war desires me to express his deep regret that your husband Corporal Marvin A. Doyle has been reported missing in action since six November over Yugoslavia if further details or other information are received you will be promptly notified. Dunlop Acting the Adjutant General." This confused Anne because Marvin's middle initial was wrong. It should have been W for Wesley. Additionally, his rank was sergeant, not corporal. Anne wasn't sure what to make of it. It would be more than two months before she heard anything else.

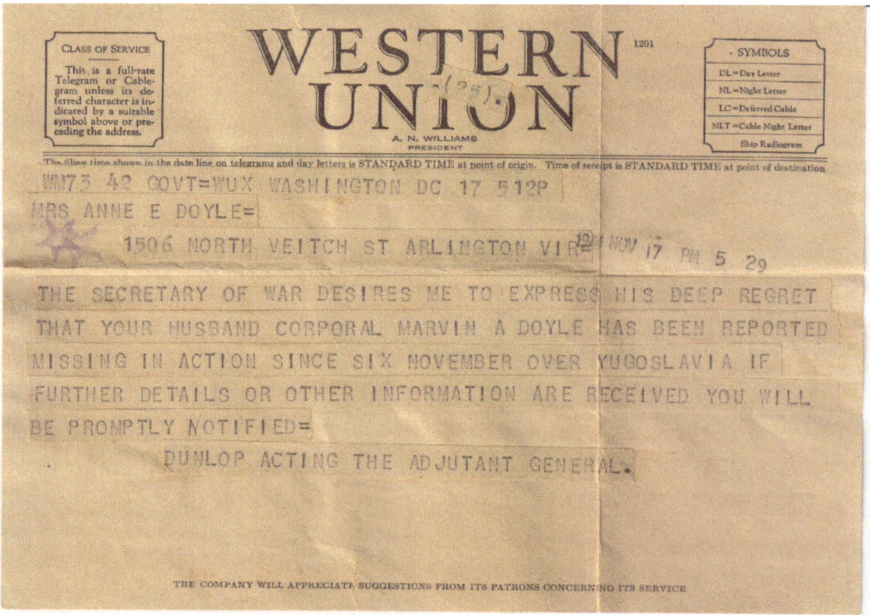

The Germans had seven prison camps called Stalag Luft which translates in English to Permanent Camps for Airmen. Stalag Luft 1 was located the farthest north by the Baltic Sea. In his diary, Marvin described the pain of the relentless cold which could reach thirty degrees below zero. The village of Barth was a strip of land that jutted out toward the Baltic Sea about one hundred miles northwest of Berlin.

A couple of miles from the main gate sat a massive Lutheran church in the village of Barth. The prisoners could see it, and many drew pictures of it during their captivity. A large pine forest was on the west side of the camp and even though Marvin thought they were a few miles from the sea, it was much closer at less than a mile from the camp.

Stalag Luft 1

Stalag Luft 1 was encircled with barbed wire. A guard tower and mounted machine gun sat every hundred yards, and a pair of spotlights constantly roamed the property looking for any sign of trouble. It was divided into five compounds, four of them were for prisoners which at its peak reached 9,000 men from America, Britain and Canada. The fifth was for the German soldiers.

Marvin was put in the North 3 Compound in Block 306 Room 13. He logged his roommates' names, rank, plane assignment and hometown.

The POWs called themselves "Kriegies," short for Kriegsgefangener, which is German for "prisoner of war." They called the Germans "Jerries." Marvin had a lot to learn about life here.

The Red Cross delivered packages to the POWs in compliance with the Geneva Convention. The parcels included things such as powdered milk, cartons of cigarettes, chocolate bars, soup, raisins, jam, peanut butter, prunes, cookies, cheese, coffee, sugar, biscuits, cheese, canned salmon, socks, soap and toiletries. This would supplement the German rations of bread, potatoes, and cabbage.

This particular camp was notable for a few things: an underground daily newspaper called POW WOW (Prisoners of War Waiting on Winning) secretly written and circulated through the barracks. The

Germans were suspicious over how news was getting through the camp but couldn't stop it. Those behind the newspaper had a secret radio hidden in a wall and would listen to the BBC every night to get news updates on the war. They would also interview the new prisoners coming in for the latest information, and the POWs who could speak German would eavesdrop on the guards. Their news gathering became rather sophisticated.

Another notable POW in Stalag Luft 1 was 1st Lt. Clair William Cline from Tacoma, Washington. He built a violin out of bunk bed slats and a chair. He obtained additional tools he needed by trading Red Cross rations with other prisoners. The violin was finished in time for him to play carols on Christmas Day.

The last noteworthy thing to happen here was an incredible stand-off between an American colonel and the Nazi guards as the war was about to end. The prison camp newspaper, POW WOW, was learning how United States forces were quickly approaching the camp from the west and the Russians were quickly advancing on the east. The men wondered who would arrive first and free them. The Germans began to panic and ordered all the airmen to start building sleds and prepare to evacuate Stalag Luft 1 immediately. The Senior American Officer, Colonel Hubert Zemke, refused. He was the son of German immigrants and the German he spoke was helpful. A tense showdown began between Zemke and the Nazi Commandant.

Fearing further bloodshed, the Commandant finally backed down. The Nazi guards agreed to leave and let the POWs remain in the camp. When the POWs woke up the next morning, May 1, 1945, the guards were gone. They replaced the Nazi flag with a homemade flag of stars and stripes. The very next day, the first Soviet troops arrived. But in an unexpected move, the Russian soldiers refused to free the Allied soldiers and kept the gates locked. The Nazis surrendered on May 7, 1945, but the POWs were not allowed to evacuate. The prisoners were learning the Russians were allies but not friends. Almost two weeks later, a U.S. Colonel arrived and threatened to shoot the Soviet Commander if he didn't release the men. The gates were finally opened to freedom.

Amid those more well-known happenings at Stalag Luft 1 was a quiet man who didn't know if he'd make it home alive. Marvin Doyle watched Red Cross cigarettes being used to barter between the POWs and bribe German guards. But he decided to use them for something else. He collected the paper wrappers from the cigarettes and wrote a diary on the backs of them. There would be thirty-seven pages to his secret journal. He could only hope Anne would one day get his journal and learn the hardship he endured.

On January 27, 1945, Anne received a second Western Union telegram which said, "Report just received through the International Red Cross that your husband Corporal Marvin W Doyle is a prisoner of the German government." The relief of knowing he was alive was quickly overtaken with devastation and worry.

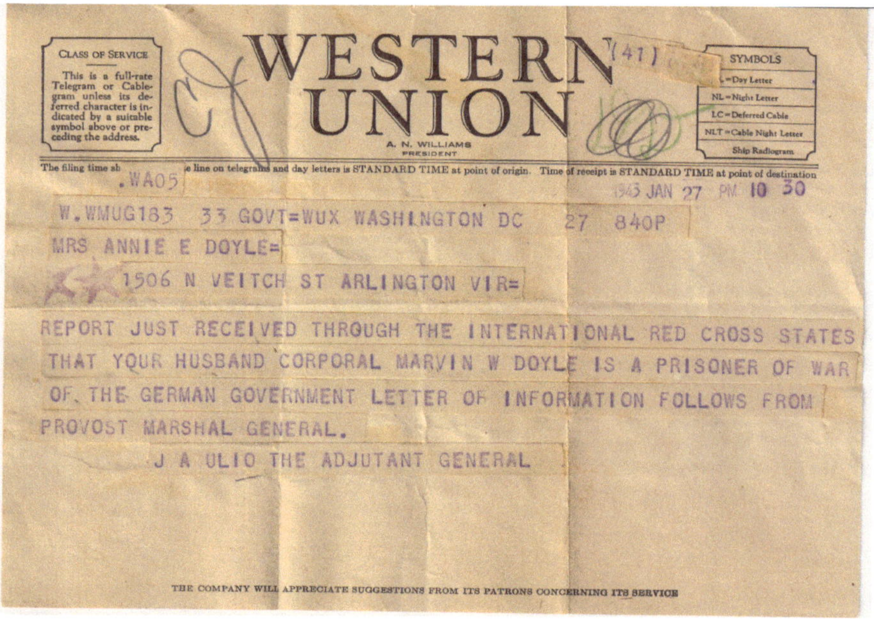

Marvin wanted Anne to know that thoughts of her kept him going. He was determined to survive to be with her again. This is Marvin's story, in his own words, never before publicly told.

Dulag-Luft. **Kriegsgefangenenkartei.**

Gefangenen-Erkennungsmarke	Dulag-Luft Eingeliefert
Nr. 6694	am: 11.12.44 L.

NAME: DOYLE

Vornamen: Marvin

Dienstgrad: Sgt.   Funktion: G.

Matrikel-No.: 33 636 258

Geburtstag: 28.1.11

Geburtsort: Oklahoma City

Religion: p.

Zivilberuf: Arbeiter   *Bauarbeiter*

Staatsangehörigkeit: USA

Vorname des Vaters: *Walter*

Familienname der Mutter: +

Verheiratet mit: ja

Anzahl der Kinder: *1*

Heimatanschrift:

Mrs. A. E. Doyle
1506 -N-Veitch Str.
Arlington Va.

Abschuß am: 6.11.44 bei: Mostar *Jugoslav.* Flugzeugtyp: B 24

Gefangennahme am: " bei: " *durch Flak*

Nähere Personalbeschreibung

Figur: schlank

Größe: 1.79

Schädelform: oval

Haare: braun

Gewicht: kg 79

Gesichtsform: oval

Gesichtsfarbe: gesund

Augen: blau

Nase: gerade

Bart:

Gebiß: gesund

Besondere Kennzeichen: *nicht verwundet.*

Rechter Zeigefinger

Front   Profil   Fingerabdruck

K/0257

MARVIN DOYLE'S SECRET DIARY

What follows are images of the actual handwritten diary on the backs of cigarette packs. The images are actual size. A transcription of the entire diary is at the end of this chapter.

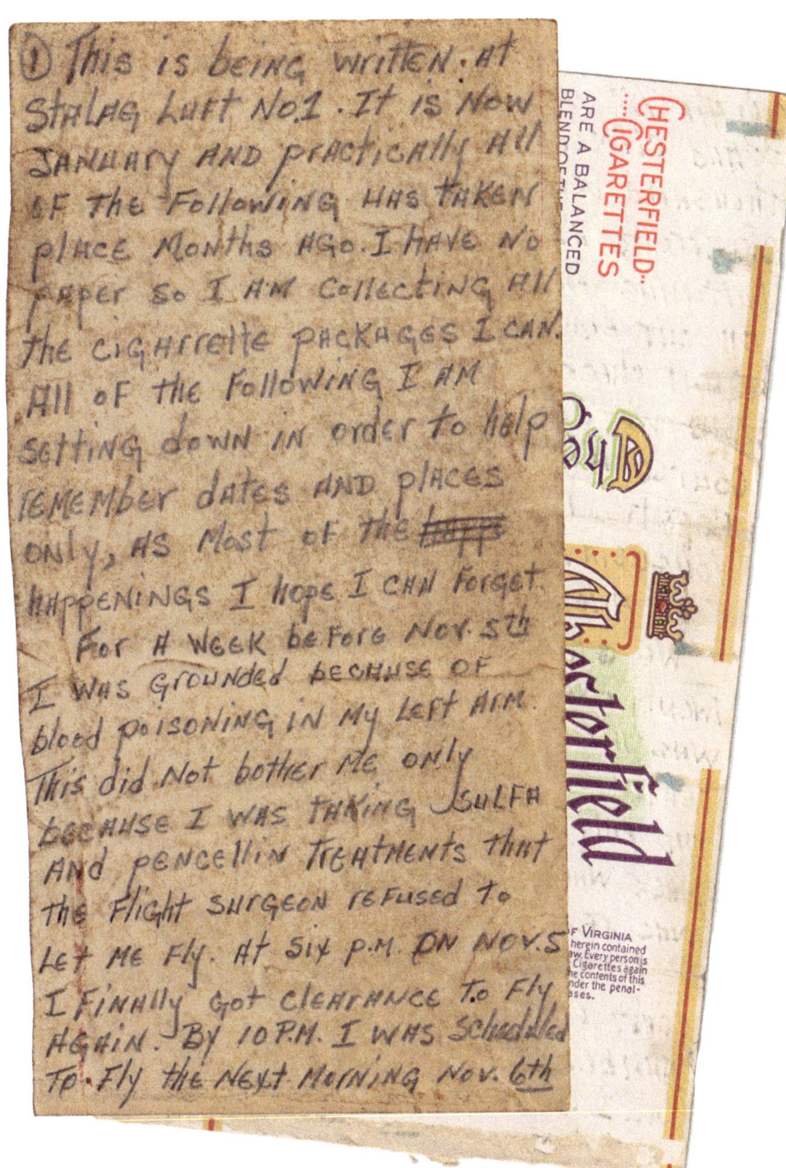

① This is being written at
Stalag Luft No.1. It is Now
January and practically all
of the following has taken
place months ago. I have no
paper so I am collecting all
the cigarrette packages I can.
All of the following I am
setting down in order to help
remember dates and places
only, as most of the happenings
happenings I hope I can forget.
    For a week before Nov. 5th
I was grounded because of
blood poisoning in my left arm.
This did not bother me only
because I was taking sulfa
and pencellin Treatments that
the flight surgeon refused to
let me fly. At six p.m. on Nov. 5
I finally got clearance to fly
again. By 10 P.M. I was scheduled
to fly the next morning Nov. 6th

CHESTERFIELD
CIGARETTES
ARE A BALANCED
BLEND OF THE

Chesterfield

OF VIRGINIA
hergin contained
aw. Every person is
Cigarettes again
he contents of this
nder the penal-
ses.

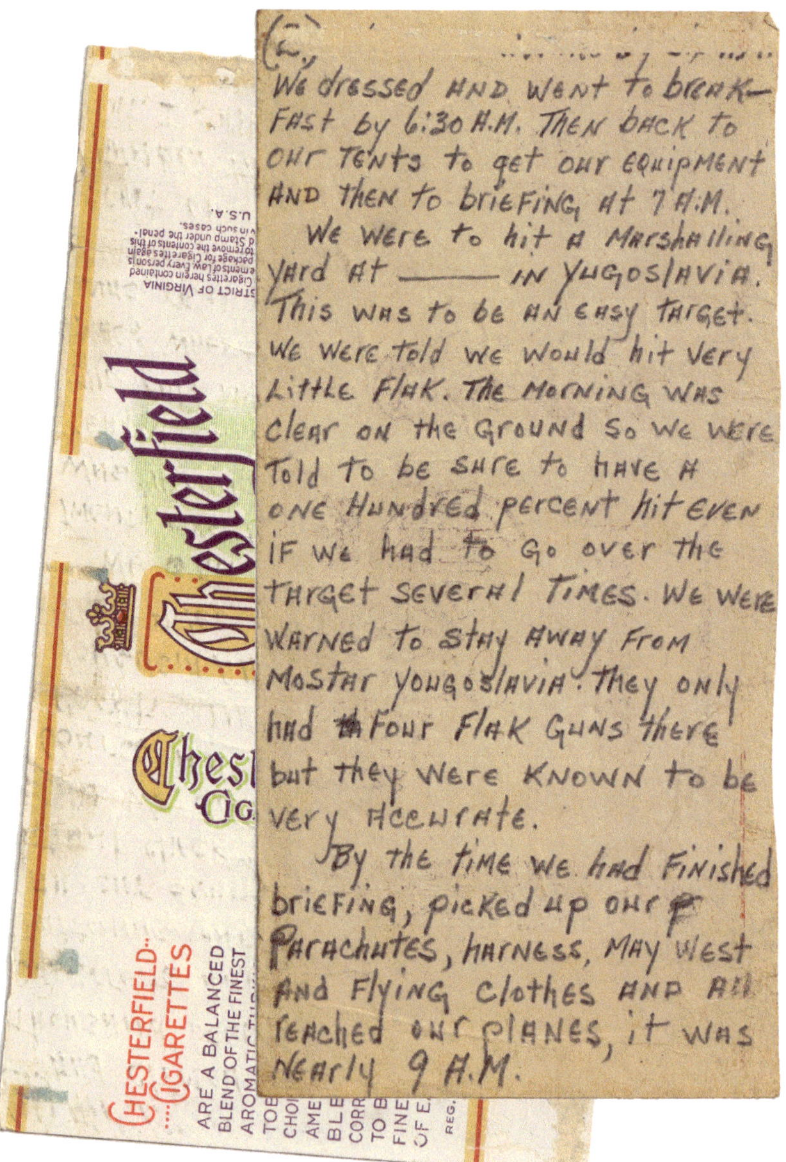

(3) We had been assigned ship number 165 an old ship that had been on over one hundred missions. It was a rule on our field that the engineer had to be in the upper Martin Turret. This made me have to move to the left waist window. The ship we were flying being an old model, we had open waist windows. We were to bomb from twenty one thousand feet with ten - five hundred pound bombs so we knew we were due for a cold ride in the waist. # We checked all of our positions and warmed our motors and were ready to taxi by ten A.M. We had been assigned number six position in Baker two box. We were flying with only three boxes for this mission all three boxes were in the

(4.) Air by 10:30 A.M. After we had climed to about five thousand feet we had a final cigarrette and then finished buttoning our clothes and gave all our equipment and guns a final check before it was too cold. We continned climing on course all the way across the Adratic in order to hit the Yongoslavia coast around four miles up.

We hit our initial I.P. at about twenty one thousand feet and it was around thirty below zero. My heated suit was working perfectly and only my face around my oxygen mask where it froze to my face was really cold.

Just as we crossed over the coast of Yougo I noticed that our number three motor was throwing oil. I called our pilot and he

5]. Told me to watch it and report
if it started leaking very bad.
It meant asking for trouble if
we had to leave the formation
and stragle back by our selves
as enemy fighters would hit
us sure. McVay was flying the
right waist - Steffano in the
ball and Rinne was in the
tail. Pruvenok was in the nose
and Matusavich in the upper.
Upon crossing our I.P. We
all put on our flak suits, They
are made with small plates of
flexible steel and cover a mans
shoulders - chest and back down
to the waist. These suits weigh
about forty pounds and over all
our other equipment made a total
of about 100 Lbs of equipment.
Number three continued to leak
but did not seem to get any
worse. We hit our bomb run at
twenty one thousand.

6. ~~our~~ Kearns our pilot called over the interphone to have a final check with all positions. We went over our target and hit a cloud bank just as we were over it. Our lead plane did not release his bombs so as we still had not run into any flak we went over and made a 360° and started our second run.

Just as we started in on our second run No. 3 caught fire. I called the pilot and he released one container of carbon dioxide. This put out the flame but our prop governor went out and the engine started racing at full throttle. Kearns tried to feather the prop but it was impossible.

By this time we were almost over our target again. The nose gunner called flak at twelve o'clock and then hell broke

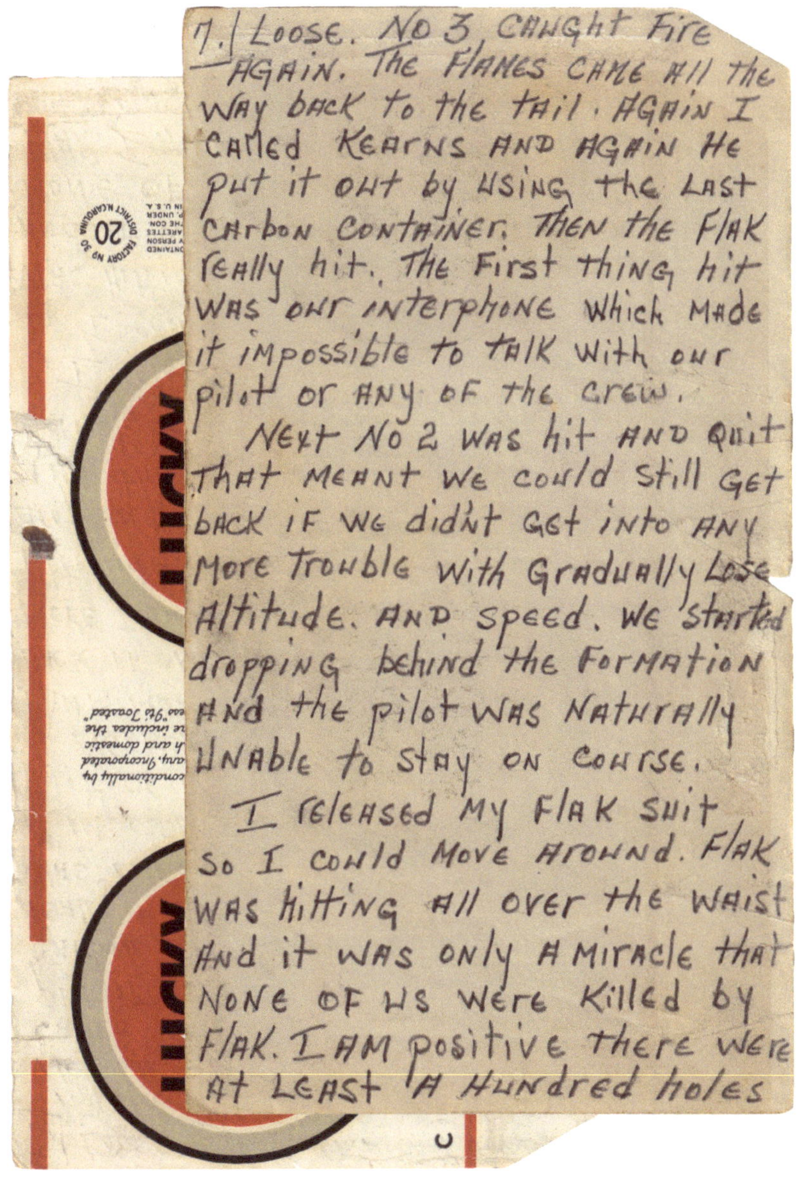
7. Loose. No 3 caught fire
again. The flames came all the
way back to the tail. Again I
called Kearns and again he
put it out by using the last
carbon container. Then the flak
really hit. The first thing hit
was our interphone which made
it impossible to talk with our
pilot or any of the crew.
    Next No 2 was hit and quit
That meant we could still get
back if we didn't get into any
more trouble with gradually lose
altitude. and speed. We started
dropping behind the formation
and the pilot was naturally
unable to stay on course.
    I released my flak suit
so I could move around. Flak
was hitting all over the waist
and it was only a miracle that
none of us were killed by
flak. I am positive there were
at least a hundred holes

8| That I could have counted from my position. All this time we were drifting off course and had lost our formation. We began to get clear of the flak, but were losing altitude fast and still had our bombs. We let our bombs go over some mountains but we still lost altitude.

Our nose gunner came back into the waist to tell us to strip the ship. We threw out everything we possibly could rip loose. All at once flak started again. (We later learned we had drifted over Mostar. This was the town we had been warned about) True they only had four batteries of flak guns there but also they were very good. I think all four guns hit us. The flak sounded

(9) LiKe HAil oN A tiN roof
As it hit us. No. 3 burst into
FlAME AGAIN. NeXt FLAK hit NO
1 Motor. I cAlled AtteNtioN OF
the rest of the boys iN the WAist
To this AND WE All Got our
pArAchutes SNApped. oN The
TAil GuNNer Got out of his
Turrett AND LAyed dowN oN the
CAtWAlk betweeN the WAist AND
TAil. FlAK WAs so thick it LooKed
Like you could WAlk From oNe
burst to ANother. WE HAd dropped
to A Height of About three Miles
up wheN the co-pilot stuck his
HeAd iN From the bomb bAy door
AND yelled For us to Get the
Hell out of there. I reAched
For the escApe HAtch door iN the
Floor AND the ball GuNNer HAd
LeFt his Turrett AND WAS StANdiNG
oN it. It seeMed LiKe AGes but
WAs probAly oNly A secoNd before
I could MAKe him uNderstANd As

10] he hadn't heard the co-pilot yell to us. I finally got him off and opened the door. Just as I got it open a burst of flak came in and went through the top of the ship. McVay went through first to be followed immediatly by the nose gunner Pruvenok. Steffano the ball gunner hesitated a couple seconds and then jumped.

I turned to look for Rinnig our tail gunner and found he was still laying in the catwalk. He had become so afraid he had frozen with fear. I managed to get back to him and get him up. I shoved him back to the door and made him understand he had to jump. For a second he refused, then he smiled and out he went. The ship went into a bank and I knew

11.) that the pilot had lost his seat. Just as I started to jump I remembered a pack of cigarettes I had wedged under my gun mount. I went back and got them and then went to the door and out. Flak was still thick so I dropped free for about a thousand feet before I pulled my cord. I got a pretty good jolt but did'nt black out.

I could only count six chutes, five below and one just above me. Some were already on the ground. The one above and near was my pilot He and I had jumped at about the same time. (I learned later the engineer was first, followed by the bombadier and the navigator and then the co-pilot, and then those of us in the waist as I have named them).

As soon as my chute opened there was no sensation of fall.

(2) All the territory below was rocky AND MountAinous. There was Just A Little wind blowing. At First I thought I would hit in the Mountains but soon I knew the wind would carry me into A Valley, Also I was headed straight For A river. I spilt my chute Twice to miss the river And hit in the rocks on the bank. My Left Ankle folded up AND All I could do was get my chute off To Keep it From dragging me.

There were About A hundred German Soldiers on Top oF me in Less than A halF Minute. I Fully Expected For one oF them To Shoot me Any Second All I could do was to raise My hands Any Move to reach My 45 would have been Fatal.

One oF them Took My Gun And then they Took About All I had. My pocketbook - watch

13| Fountain pen-, helmet and
scarf also my cigarettes and the
escape kit each man carried. Then
they made me hobble to a house
about a hundred yards away.
Here they set me against a wall
and took off my flying boot and
looked at my ankle and laughed
Then one German who could speak
broken English threw my boot
back at me and said something
about Americans liking to die
with thier boots on. I thought
sure that was it. Just as I put
my boot on a German officer
came up on a motorcycle and
took charge of me. His arrival
probably saved my life.
     He put me in a sidecar and
took me to a building about a
mile away. Here I joined my pilot
and co-pilot. My pilot was unhurt
but my co-pilot had been drug by
his chute in the rocks and had
two bad scalp wounds. This Turned
out to be a sub headquarters

14) They kept us here for a couple hours trying to get information. It was here that I soon learned that our tail gunner was dead. He must have been too afraid to open his chute. We were taken to head quarters in the town of Mostar. Here we were kept until about 6 P.M. Also here we joined the rest of our crew.

We were then moved to what had been the local jail. Here we were put in a basement room with nothing but a bare floor. We were below ground level and the windows were broken and it was awfully cold.

About eight P.M. we were given a piece of black German bread for our first to eat since early that morning. In the morning we were given quart tins that were rusty

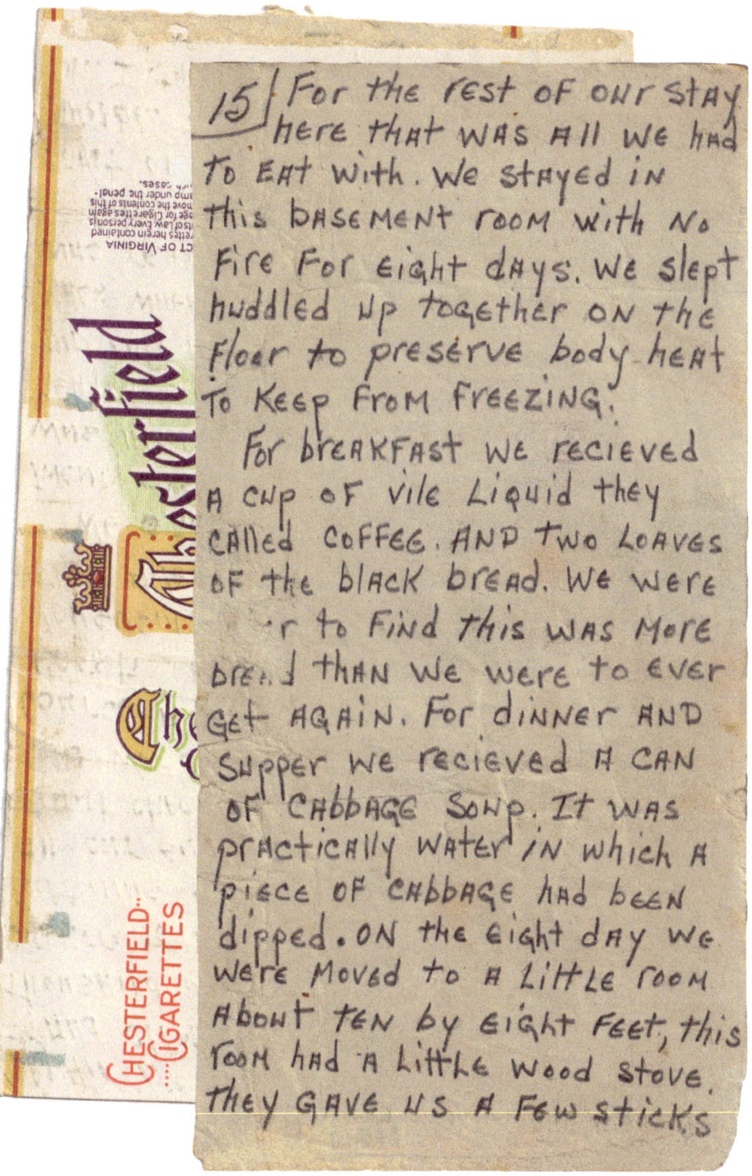

15| For the rest of our stay here that was all we had to eat with. We stayed in this basement room with no fire for eight days. We slept huddled up together on the floor to preserve body heat to keep from freezing.

For breakfast we recieved a cup of vile liquid they called coffee. And two loaves of the black bread. We were ...r to find this was more bread than we were to ever get again. For dinner and supper we recieved a can of cabbage soup. It was practically water in which a piece of cabbage had been dipped. On the eight day we were moved to a little room about ten by eight feet, this room had a little wood stove. They gave us a few sticks

16| of wood a day. this helped
A little but only the man
sleeping next to the stove got any
heat as all the heat went up the
chimney. on the 16th of Nov. which
was my 13th wedding anniversary
About Noon we were told we were
being moved to Sarajevo about
30 Miles away. about one o'clock
~~there~~ we had an air raid and
were unable to get there as
our boys had bombed the ...

The Next Morning (17th) they
got us up at Four A.M. and
loaded us in a truck and gave
us two loaves of bread. We ~~traveled~~
Traveled for 13 hrs in the Mountains
in order to make the 30 Miles.

At Sarajevo we were again
put in a bare room about 20 x 20
on the third floor of a building
only 2 blocks away from the
Marshalling yard that had
been our target. we stayed
in this room 13 days until
the 30th of Nov.

17 | Here we still had our tin cans to eat from. For these 13 days we were given a tin of that same vile coffee and each man. Got a piece of bread which was about the size of three slices which was to last all day. For dinner and supper we got a tin of soup. One meal would be cabbage soup the next meal some kind of bean. None of us ever found more than eight beans in a tin the rest being hot water and bugs. Yes the beans had a bug that looked like our potato bugs. For several days we threw this soup away. But believe it or not we soon were so hungry we ate it bugs and all. We had eaten so little since being down that outside of getting rid of water from the soup we only used the toilet about once every five days.

Lack of food was'nt our biggest worry. The Marshalling yard only

18/ Two blocks away was still being bombed by our boys every day and some time twice a day. There were Air raid shelters under our building and everyone but us spent hours each day in these. The Germans left us locked in our room hoping our own boys would drop a bomb on us. We could see the bombs on the way down and they would hit and rock the room. All we could do was to sit and hope our boys were on the ball and didn't miss thier Target.

This is enough about our stay in Sarajevo. It was plenty rough but we were to learn that we still had worse to come.

On the 30th of Nov. we were awakened at 6A.M. and told we were to move again. Each man recieved a loaf of bread, a piece of sweet butter about twice the size of that you would get in a restaurant in the U.S.

19| Also a piece of German beef about the size of a package of cigarettes. This was to last us three days. We left Sarejevo about seven A.M. (Nov 30th). We were put in a box car and given guards with full packs weighing about seventy pounds which we were made to carry. We only travelled about an hour when we reached a bombed out bridge. Here we carried the German packs about two miles down stream in the cold and mud and crossed the river by a boat tied to a cable strung across the river. I thought I wouldn't make it as my ankle was still awfully swollen and sore. We had to wait on the other side for another train. This time we we were put on a flat car in the rain. The trains never travelled over 8 miles per hour

20. At night we were fired upon by partasans. Of course we knew they were trying to help the Allies but that was little comfort with shells flying. It took us 4 days to reach Brod Yougo. So the fourth day we didn't eat. At Brod the railway was bombed out so they took us 3 miles to a prison. Again we carried the German packs.

Here we were put in an old wine cellar. It was awfully cold and damp. We only spent one night and two days. We still got a tin of coffee for breakfast and soup for the other two meals. The night of the second day we again walked to the train and

21. AGAIN GIVEN THE SAME
RATIONS FOR THREE DAYS.
THIS TIME WE WERE PUT ON A
COACH BUT ALL THE WINDOWS
WERE BROKEN AND IT WAS
TERRIBLY COLD. THIS TRIP STARTED
ON THE NIGHT OF DEC 5th.
WE ARRIVED IN VIENNA ON THE
MORNING OF THE 7th. HERE WE
CAUGHT A STREETCAR AND RODE
ACROSS TOWN TO ANOTHER STATION.
VIENNA HAD BEEN A BEAUTIFUL
CITY BEFORE OUR BOMBERS HAD
PAID THEM A FEW VISITS. WE
GOT RATIONS AGAIN AND AGAIN
ON A COACH WITH NO WINDOWS
WE STARTED OUT FOR AGRAM ALSO
IN YOUGO. WE ONLY HAD THREE
DAYS RATIONS AND THIS TIME
IT TOOK US FIVE DAYS SO WE
WENT HUNGRY AS WELL AS COLD
FOR TWO DAYS. AGAIN AT AGRAM
WE WALKED ABOUT TWO MILES

22] To another prison. We spent
one night there and the next
morning at three A.M. We started
for Frankford on the Main.
Enroute we were strafed by
Russian fighter pilots flying
American P-51. Nine passengers
were killed but again we were
spared. We arrived at Frankford
on the morning of Dec 11th
Here we were again taken by
streetcar to another prison. Here
we got a shower and allowed
to shave and then were put in
solitaire for the rest of the day
and night. We were given one
slice of bread and a bowl of
soup all day. At six A.M. the
next morning we were given
a cup of coffee and one piece
of bread. We were this time
made to walk about 5 miles in
a blinding snowstorm to the
station

23 | This time we only had forty miles to go. We took over 14 hours to make this and on the night of Dec 13th about 10 P.M. we arrived at Dulag #3 in Wetzlar Germany. Here we were given a suitcase from the red cross and a hot shower.

This made a new man out of us. We recieved a pair of army shoes, a scarf, two sweaters, & 2 pr. of winter underwear, 3 pr of socks, 4 handkerchiefs. 5 packages of cigarrettes, a pipe and two pks. of pipe tobacco. One pr of pajamas. One shirt a pair of gloves and sewing kit and a pk of bandaid. and a bottle of vitamin pills.

Then even though it was nearly eleven P.M. we were given a meal We had potatoes, corned beef 4 slices of bread with butter

24/ 2 cups of American coffee and some stewed prunes. Then we were given a bed, at least we had a stove and two blankets and a sack filled with some straw.

I know I will never be able to make anyone ~~understand~~ understand how we felt after all we had been through for the past 35 days. Just to be clean and warm and not be hungry. None of us realized how much this meant before. I dont know how much the red cross helps the men in combat areas but I do know that without them the P.O.W. would have a much more miserable life.

After being at Dulag #3 for a week we were allowed to write a card home. We could only say we were alive and whether we were injured or not.

25/ We stayed here for a week. While there we ate 2 slices of bread with butter and 2 cups of American coffee for each breakfast. For dinner we had a slice of bread with butter and cheese 2 large crackers with butter and jam and mashed potatoes and 2 cups of tea. For supper one slice of bread with more potatoes with salmon mixed in them and 2 cups of cocoa. This wasn't a lot to eat but to us it seemed like heaven.

Steffano - the ball gunner had scratched his thumb and because of the poor food we had been eating it became infected and he went to the hospital with blood poisioning. Word came to the camp to send 45 N.C.O. to an officers camp to be orderlies. All of our boys volunteered and we shipped

26| out about 4 P.M on the
20th of Dec. Leaving our
ball gunner in the hospital but
the C.O. promised to send him
later. Upon leaving each two
men were given a red cross
food package. Mac and I split
one parcel. We were given one
loaf of bread for each 5 men
per day. We spent three nights
and two days on another cold
coach.

We arrived at Stalag #1
Barth Germany on the 23rd of
Dec. It was about 30° below zero
when we arrived and snow all
around. Again we walked about
three miles to our prison.

Again we were given a hot
shower and assigned twenty four
men to a room. This room was about
18'x18'. We had a small stove
2 tables and benches and 24
bunks. The bunks were three

27) high. They were only wide wooden shelves. We had a sack filled with straw, and 2 blankets. Here we were given a blouse and another pair of socks and a belt and another sewing kit.

We had to live, sleep, eat, cook and dry our clothes in the one room. We split the twenty four men into two combines of twelve men each. Two men from each combine were picked as cooks for that combine. Joe Miller and I were picked for our combine.

Each man was supposed to get one package of red cross food per week. The Germans gave us one loaf of bread a day for each six men. They also gave us a few potatoes and about once a week some

28/ SOME SUGAR AND ONCE IN A while SOME CABBAGE AND TURNIPS. WE very seldom Got our red cross packages As we were suppose too. But it Is surprising how you can stretch THINGS AND MAKE OUT without being too hungry. WE were each Given A bowl, A spoon, KNife AND Fork AND Two pitchers For coFFEE AND A Two GALLON bucket to cook in

A person Should see what the boys MANAGED to MAKE with TiN CANS AND pieces OF wire. SOME OF our boys MAde dippers AND A potato MASher. They MAde bAKiNG PANS AND WE EVEN MAde MEAT LOAF with bread CruMbS AND MEAT Also puddings with bread CruMbS AND rAiSiNS AND pruNES.

SOME TiMES For breakfast we hAd bread cereal. For br Then SANdwiches AND COFFEE For dinner AND potAtoes, MEAT AND MAybe CAbbAGE or TurNips

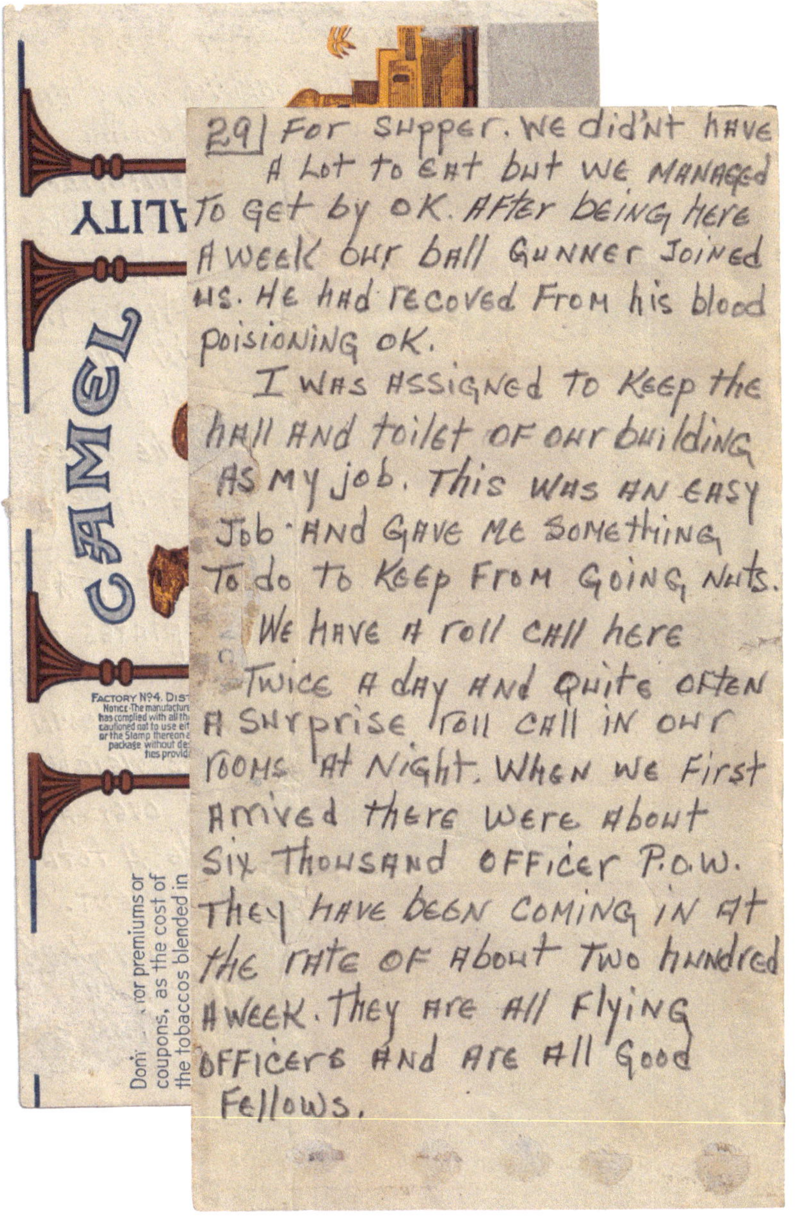

29] For supper. We did'nt have
a lot to eat but we managed
to get by ok. After being here
a week our ball gunner joined
us. He had recoved from his blood
poisioning ok.

I was assigned to keep the
hall and toilet of our building
as my job. This was an easy
job. And gave me something
to do to keep from going nuts.

We have a roll call here
twice a day and quite often
a surprise roll call in our
rooms at night. When we first
arrived there were about
six thousand officer P.o.w.
They have been coming in at
the rate of about two hundred
a week. They are all flying
officers and are all good
fellows.

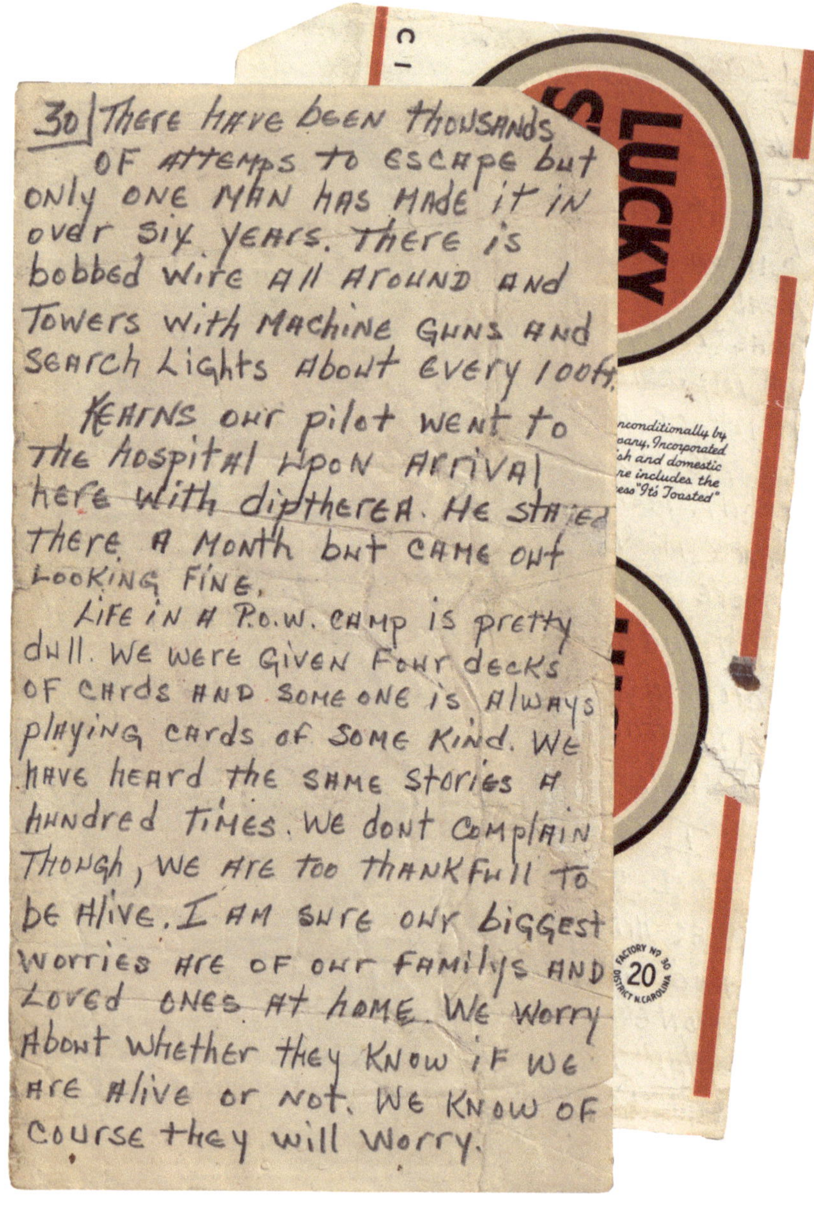
30| There have been thousands
of attemps to escape but
only one man has made it in
over six years. There is
bobbed wire all around and
Towers with machine guns and
search lights about every 100ft.

Kearns our pilot went to
the hospital upon arrival
here with diptherea. He staied
there a month but came out
looking fine.

Life in a P.O.W. camp is pretty
dull. We were given four decks
of cards and some one is always
playing cards of some kind. We
have heard the same stories a
hundred times. We dont complain
though, we are too thankfull to
be alive. I am sure our biggest
worries are of our familys and
loved ones at home. We worry
about whether they know if we
are alive or not. We know of
course they will worry.

31.| We are allowed to write
two letters and four post cards
a month, but we dont know #if.
they go through or not. We have
learned from the older fellows
that we will be here about
seven months before we get
any mail.

From the time we reached
here it has been getting colder
and colder. It gets around
50° below zero here in Feb,
We are only about four miles
from the baltic sea. Nothing
in sight but snow and ice
We can only use the inside
toilet from nine P.M. until eight
A.M. We have to walk about
a block to wash and shave
and the wind will freeze
water on your hands and face
if you dont dry carefully. A
mystery to me is why in the
world the water in the

32.! Pipes in the outside
Toilets doesn't freeze and
break the pipes. We are
allowed to keep our lights
on until ten P.M.

Then comes the tough
part for me. Every night
I lie for hours thinking
of Anne, if she is well
and worrying about me.
How Dad is getting along.
Thinking of all the things we
use to do in civilian life.
Most of all I think about
being able to go home when
this mess is all over.

I am hoping this will
be over some time in Feb
or March. It may take months
for us to get home and we
may get home in just a few
weeks. Any way or time it
does happen it will all be
worth all of this to be

33.| BACK WITH ANNE AGAIN.
I dont think I will WANT
TOO MUCH OUT OF LIFE WHEN I GET
HOME. MOST OF ALL I WANT to be
with ANNE AGAIN. THEN I WANT
MY FRiends AND A DECENT
PLACE to LiVE.

I WANT A Good bed with
pillows AND NEVER HAVE to
Go to bed HUNGRY AND COLD
AGAIN. This I think will be ALL
I REALLY NEED. I HAVE bEEN
COLD bEFORE FOR AN HOUR or SO
but I NEVER KNEW WHAT it
COULD bE LiKE to bE COLD FOR
OVER 30 DAYS.

I HAD bEEN HUNGRY I thought
but A PERSON Would HAVE to
Go FOR A MONTH LiKE WE did to
REALLY KNOW how TERRible it CAN
bE. I KNOW I HAVE REAd bEFORE
About people being HUNGRY but

34. Now I know I never realized how it really felt.

There wont be much more to this story if you can call it that. Nothing much happens here exciting. Every once in awhile the Germans pull a surprise search and if they ever find this it I will be put in Solataire on bread and water but I want to get this written down. With nothing to do your mind is bound to get dull and I dont trust mine very far, especially on dates. Of course lots of this I will never forget and will wish that I could. This part I am writing on the 25th of Jan.

Have had this hidden for some time. Have had several searches but so far this has'nt been found. The fellows made a cake and gave me a big surprise for my birthday. They used pipe cleaners and wrote happy birthday. Also on my birthday I started work as a cook.

35 | IN A NEW MESS HALL WE ONLY COOK GERMAN RATIONS, SUCH AS POTATOES AND HORSE MEAT, CABBAGE AND TURNIPS AND HEAT WATER FOR COFFEE TWICE A DAY. THIS HELPS PASS THE TIME A LOT

WE HAVE HAD SOME BAD WEATHER, SEVERAL BLIZZARDS WITH AROUND 40° BELOW ZERO. I MADE A CALANDER BACK IN NOVEMBER BUT IT ONLY GOES AS FAR AS THE END OF FEBUARY. I STILL HOPE I WONT HAVE TO ADD ANY MORE MONTHS. OUR LIGHTS AND WATER WERE OFF SEVERAL DAYS AGO. WE HAD TO MELT SNOW TO GET ANY WATER AT ALL

36 | This is being
written on the 3rd
day of Febnary. We are
still eating fair. We
are getting nearly a
package a man per
week, with a few potatos
and cabbage once in
awhile. We havent had
any new men arrive
lately. We hope it is
because Germany is
getting hard pressed for
transportation. I am still
hoping for an end to
all of this some time
this month. I may be
off by months but that
is all we can do is hope.
We were told yesterday
that we cant write or
recieve any more mail

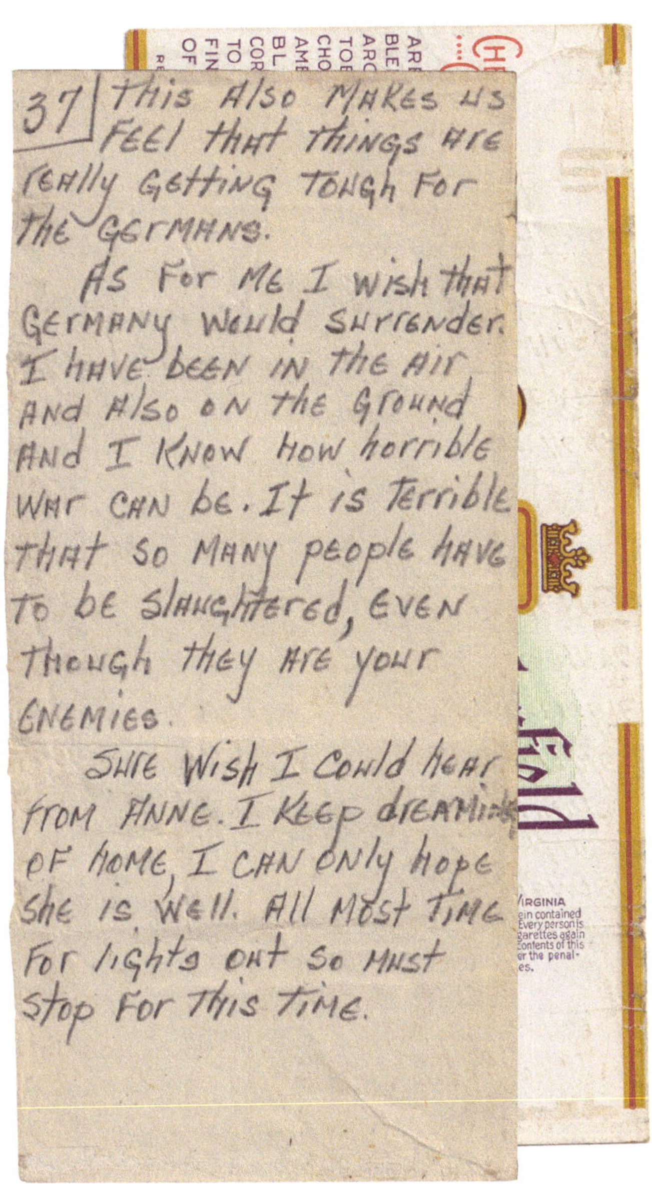

37 | This Also MAKES US
FEEL that things Are
reAlly Getting Tough For
THE GErMANS.

As For ME I wish that
GErMANy would surrender.
I hAVE been in THE Air
And Also on THE Ground
And I Know How horrible
WAr cAn be. It is Terrible
THAt So MANy people HAVE
to be SlAughTered, EVEN
Though they Are your
ENEMIES.

SHrE Wish I could Hear
FroM ANNE. I Keep dreAMing
of HOME, I cAn only hope
she is well. All Most TIME
For lights ouT so Must
stop For This TIME.

Following is a verbatim transcription of Marvin's handwritten diary. The text has not been edited for grammar, punctuation or format.

1. This is being written at Stalag Luft No 1. It is now January and practically all of the following has taken place months ago. I have no paper so I am collecting all the cigarette packages I can. All of the following I am setting down in order to help remember dates and places only, as most of the happenings I hope I can forget.
   For a week before Nov. 5th I was grounded because of blood poisoning in my left arm. This did not bother me only because I was taking sulfa and penicillin treatments that the flight surgeon refused to let me fly. At six p.m. on Nov 5 I finally got clearance to fly again. By 10 P.M. I was scheduled to fly the next morning Nov. 6th.

2. We dressed and went to breakfast by 6:30 A.M. then back to our tents to get our equipment and then to briefing at 7 A.M.
   We were to hit a marshaling yard at _________ in Yugoslavia. This was to be an easy target. We were told we would hit very little flak. The morning was clear on the ground so we were told to be sure to have a one hundred percent hit even if we had to go over the target several times. We were warned to stay away from Mostar, Yugoslavia. They only had four flak guns there but they were known to be very accurate.
   By the time we had finished briefing, picked up our parachutes, harness, May West and flying clothes and all reached our planes, it was nearly 9 A.M.

3. We had been assigned ship number 165 an old ship that had been on over one hundred missions. It was a rule on our field that the engineer has to be in the upper martin turret. This made me have to move to the left waist window. The ship we were flying being an old model, we had open waist windows. We were to bomb from twenty one thousand feet with ten - five hundred pound bombs so we knew we were due for a cold ride in the waist.

We checked all of our positions and warmed our motors and were ready to taxi by ten A.M. We had been assigned number six position in Baker two box. We were flying with only three boxes for this mission.

All three boxes were in the

4. Air by 10:30 A.M. after were had climbed to about five thousand feet we had a final cigarette and then finished buttoning our clothes and gave all our equipment and guns a final check before it was too cold. We continued climbing on course all the way across the Adriatic in order to hit the Yugoslavia coast around four miles up.

   We hit our initial I.P. at about twenty one thousand feet and it was around thirty below zero. My heated suit was working perfectly and only my face around my oxygen mask where it froze to my face was really cold.

   Just as we crossed over the coast of Yougo I noticed that our number three motor was throwing oil. I called our pilot and he

5. Told me to watch it and report if it started leaking very bad. It meant asking for trouble if we had to leave the formation and straggle back by ourselves as enemy fighters would hit us sure. McVay was flying the right waist. Staffano in the ball and Rinne was in the tail. Pruvenok was in the nose and Matusavich in the upper.

   Upon crossing our I.P. we all put on our flak suits. They are made with small plates of flexible steel and cover a man's shoulders - chest and back down to the waist. These suits weigh about forty pounds and over all our other equipment made a total of about 100 lbs of equipment.

   Number three continued to leak but did not seem to get any worse. We hit our bomb run at twenty one thousand.

6. Kearns our pilot called over the inter phone to have a final check with all positions. We went over our target and hit a cloud bank just as we were over it. Our lead plane did not release his bombs

so as we still had not run into any flak we went over and made a 360° and started our second run.

Just as we started in on our second run No. 3 caught fire. I called the pilot and he released one container of carbon dioxide. This put out the flame but our prop governor went out and the engine started racing at full throttle. Kearns tried to feather the prop but it was impossible.

By this time we were almost over our target again. The nose gunner called flak at twelve o'clock and then hell broke

7. Loose. No. 3 caught fire again. The flames came all the way back to the tail. Again I called Kearns and again he put it out by using the last carbon container. Then the flak really hit. The first thing hit was our interphone which made it impossible to talk with our pilot or any of the crew.

Next no 2 was hit and quit that meant we could still get back if we didn't get into any more trouble with gradually lose altitude and speed. We started dropping behind the formation and the pilot was naturally unable to stay on course.

I released my flak suit so I could move around. Flak was hitting all over the waist and it was only a miracle that none of us were killed by flak. I am positive there were at least a hundred holes

8. That I could have counted from my position. All this time we were drifting off course and had lost our formation. We began to get clear of the flak, but were losing altitude fast and still had our bombs. We let our bombs go over some mountains but we still lost altitude.

Our nose gunner came back into the waist to tell us to strip the ship. We threw out everything we possibly could rip loose. All at once flak started again. (We later learned we had drifted over Mostar. This was the town we had been warned about)

True they only had four batteries of flak guns there but also they were very good. I think all four guns hit us. The flak sounded

9. Like hail on a tin roof as it hit us. No 3 burst into flame again. Next flak hit No 1 motor. I called attention of the rest of the boys in the waist to this and we all got our parachutes snapped on the tail gunner got out of his turret and laid down on the catwalk between the waist and the tail. Flak was so thick it looked like you could walk from one burst to another. We had dropped to a height of about three miles up when the co-pilot stuck his head in from the bomb bay door and yelled for us to get the hell out of there. I reached for the escape hatch door in the floor and the ball gunner had left his turret and was standing on it. It seemed like ages but was probably only a second before I could make him understand as

10. He hadn't heard the copilot yell to us. I finally got him off and opened the door. Just as I got it open a burst of flak came in and went through the top of the ship. McVay went through first to be followed immediately by the nose gunner Pruvenok. Staffano the ball gunner hesitated a couple seconds and then jumped.
    I turned to look for Rinnie our tail gunner and found he was laying in the catwalk. He had become so afraid he had frozen with fear. I managed to get back to him and get him up. I shoved him back to the door and made him understand he had to jump. For a second he refused, then he smiled and out he went. The ship went into a bank and I knew

11. The pilot had left his seat. Just as I started to jump I remembered a pack of cigarettes I had wedged under my gun mount. I went back and got them and then went to the door and out. Flak was still thick so I dropped free for about a thousand feet before I pulled my cord. I got a pretty good jolt but didn't black out.
    I could only count six chutes five below and one just above me. Some were already on the ground. The one above and near was my pilot he and I had jumped at about the same time. (I learned later the engineer was first followed by the bombardier and the navigator and then to copilot, and then those of us in the waist as

I have named them)

As soon as my chute opened there was no sensation of fall.

12. All the territory below was rocky and mountainous. There was just a little wind blowing. At first I thought I would hit in the mountains but soon I knew the wind would carry me into a valley, also I was headed straight for a river. I spilt my chute twice to miss the river and hit in the rocks on the bank. My left ankle folded up and all I could do was get my chute off to keep it from dragging me.

There were about a hundred German soldiers on top of me in less than a half a minute. I fully expected for one of them to shoot me any second all I could do was to raise my hands any move to reach my 45 would have been fatal.

One of them took my gun and then they took about all I had. My pocketbook - watch

13. Fountain pen - helmet and scarf also my cigarettes and the escape kit each man carried. Then they made me hobble to a house about a hundred yards away. Here they set me against a wall and took off my flying boot and looked at my ankle and laughed. Then one German who could speak broken English threw my boot back at me and said something about Americans liking to die with their boots on. I thought sure that was it. Just as I put my boot on a German officer came up on a motorcycle and took charge of me. His arrival probably saved my life.

He put me in a sidecar and took me to a building about a mile away. Here I joined my pilot and co-pilot. My pilot was unhurt but my copilot had been drug by his chute in the rocks and had two bad scalp wounds. This turned out to be a sub headquarters

14. They kept us here for a couple of hours trying to get information. It was here that I soon learned that our tail gunner was dead. He must have been too afraid to open his chute. We were taken to headquarters in the town of Mostar. Here we were kept until about 6 P.M. also here we joined the rest of our crew.

We were then moved to what had been the local jail. Here we were put in a basement room with nothing but a bare floor we were below ground level and the windows were broken and it was awfully cold.

About eight P.M. we were given a piece of black German bread for our first to eat since early that morning. In the morning we were given quart tins that were rusty

15. For the rest of our stay here that was all we had to eat with. We stayed in this basement room with no fire for eight days. We slept huddled up together on the floor to preserve body heat to keep from freezing.

For breakfast we received a cup of vile liquid they called coffee and two loaves of the black bread we were (later) to find this was more bread than we were to ever get again. For dinner and supper we received a can of cabbage soup. It was practically water in which a piece of cabbage had been dipped. On the eight day we were moved to a little room about ten by eight feet, this room had a little wood stove. They gave us a few sticks

16. Of wood a day. This helped a little but only the man sleeping next to the stove got any heat as all the heat went up the chimney. On the 16th of Nov which was my 13th wedding anniversary about noon we were told we were being moved to Sarajevo about 30 miles away. About one o'clock we had an air raid and were unable to get there as our boys had bombed the ________.

The next morning (17th) they got us up at four A.M. and loaded us in a truck and gave us two loaves of bread. We traveled for 13 hrs in the mountains in order to make the 30 miles.

At Sarajevo we were again put in a bare room about 20 x 20 on the third floor of a building only 2 blocks away from the marshaling yard that had been our target. We stayed in this room 13 days until the 30th of Nov.

17. Here we still had our tin cans to eat from. For these 13 days we were given a tin of that same vile coffee and each man got a

piece of bread which was about the size of three slices which was to last all day. For dinner and supper we got a tin of soup. One meal would be cabbage soup the next meal some kind of bread. None of us ever found more than eight beans in a tin the rest being hot water and bugs. Yes the beans had a bug that looked like our potato bugs. For several days we threw this soup away, but believe it or not we soon were so hungry we ate it bugs and all. We had eaten so little since being down that outside of getting rid of water from the soup we only used the toilet about once every five days.

Lack of food wasn't our biggest worry. The marshaling yard only

18. Two blocks away was still being bombed by our boys every day and some time twice a day. There were air raid shelters under our building and everyone but us spent hours each day in these. The Germans left us locked in our room hoping our own boys would drop a bomb on us. We could see the bombs on the way down and they would hit and rock the room. All we could do was to sit and hope our boys were on the ball and didn't miss their target.

This is enough about our story in Sarajevo. It was plenty rough but we were to learn that we still had worse to come.

On the 30th of Nov we were awakened at 6A.M. and told we were to move again. Each man received a loaf of bread, a piece of sweet butter about twice the size of that you would get in a restaurant in the U.S.

19. Also a piece of German beef about the size of a package of cigarettes. This was to last us three days. We left Sarajevo about seven A.M. (Nov 30th). We were put in a box car and given guards with full packs weighing about seventy pounds which we were made to carry. We only travelled about an hour when we reached a bombed out bridge. Here we carried the German packs about two miles downstream in the cold and mud and crossed the river by a boat tied to a cable strung across the river. I thought I wouldn't make it as my ankle was still awfully swollen and sore.

We had to wait on the other side for another train. This time we were put on a flat car in the rain. The trains never travelled over 8 miles per hour.

20. At night we were fired upon by partisans of course we knew they were trying to help the allies but that was little comfort with shells flying. It took us 4 days to reach Brod Yougo so the fourth day we didn't eat. At Brod the railway was bombed out so they took us 3 miles to a prison. Again we carried the German packs.

Here we were put in an old wine cellar. It was awfully cold and damp. We only spent one night and two days. We still got a tin of coffee for breakfast and soup for the other two meals. The night of the second day we again walked to the train and

21. Again given the same rations for three days. This time we were put on a coach but all the windows were broken and it was terribly cold. This trip started on the night of Dec 5th. We arrived in Vienna on the morning of the 7th. Here we caught a streetcar and rode across town to another station. Vienna had been a beautiful city before our bombers had paid them a few visits. We got rations again and again on a coach with no windows. We started out for Agram also in Yougo, we only had three days rations and this time it took us five days so we went hungry as well as cold for two days. Again at Agram we walked about two miles

22. To another prison. We spent one night there and the next morning at three A.M. we started for Frankford on the main.

Enroute we were strafed by Russian fighter pilots flying American P-51. Nine passengers were killed but again we were spared. We arrived at Frankford on the morning of Dec 11th. Here we were again taken by streetcar to another prison. Here we got a shower and allowed to shave and then were put in solitaire for the rest of the day and night. We were given one slice of bread and a bowl of soup all day. At six A.M. the next morning we were given a cup of coffee and one piece of bread. We were this time made to walk about 5 miles in a blinding snowstorm to the station.

23. This time we only had forty miles to go. We took over 14 hours to make this and on the night of Dec 13th about 10 P.M. we arrived at Dulag 3 in Wetzlar, Germany. Here we were given a suitcase from the red cross and a hot shower.

    This made a new man out of us. We received a pair of army shoes, a scarf, two sweaters, 2pr of winter underwear, 3 pr of socks, 4 handkerchiefs, 5 packages of cigarettes, a pipe and two pks of pipe tobacco, one pr of pajamas, one shirt, a pair of gloves and sewing kit and a pk of bandaid and a bottle of vitamin pills.

    Then even though it was nearly eleven P.M. we were given a meal. We had potatoes, corned beef 4 slices of bread with butter

24. 2 cups of American coffee and some stewed prunes. Then we were given a bed, at least we had a stove and two blankets and a sack filled with some straw.

    I know I will never be able to make anyone understand how we felt after all we had been through for the past 35 days. Just to be clean and warm and not be hungry. None of us realized how much this meant before. I don't know how much the red cross helps the men in combat areas but I do know that without them the P.O.W. would have a much more miserable life.

    After being at Dulag #3 for a week we were allowed to write a card home. We could only say we were alive and whether we were injured or not.

25. We stayed here for a week. While there we ate 2 slices of bread with butter and 2 cups of American coffee for each breakfast. For dinner we had a slice of bread with butter and cheese 3 large crackers with butter and jam and mashed potatoes and 2 cups of tea. For supper one slice of bread with more potatoes with salmon mixed in them and 2 cups of cocoa. This wasn't a lot to eat but to us it seemed like heaven.

    Steffano - the ball gunner had scratched his thumb and because of the poor food we had been eating it became infected and he went to the hospital with blood poisoning. Word came to the camp to send 45 N.C.O. to an officers camp to be orderlies. All of our boys volunteered and we shipped

26. Out about 4 P.M. on the 20th of Dec leaving our ball gunner in the hospital but the C.O. promised to send him later. Upon leaving each two men were given a red cross food package. Mac and I split one parcel. We were given one loaf of bread for each 5 men per day. We spent three nights and two days on another cold coach.

We arrived at Stalag #1 Barth, Germany on the 23rd of Dec. it was about 30 degrees below zero when we arrived and snow all around. Again we walked about three miles to our prison.

Again we were given a hot shower and assigned twenty four men to a room. This room was about 18′ x 18′. We had a small stove 2 tables and benches and 24 bunks. The bunks were three

27. High. They were only wide wooden shelves. We had a sack filled with straw, and 2 blankets. Here we were given a blouse and another pair of socks and a belt and another sewing kit.

We had to live, sleep, eat, cook and dry our clothes in the one room. We split the twenty four men into two combines of twelve men each. Two men from each combine were picked as cooks for that combine. Joe Miller and I were picked for our combine.

Each man was supposed to get one package of red cross food per week. The Germans gave us one loaf of bread a day for each six men. They also gave us a few potatoes and about once a week some

28. Some sugar and once in a while some cabbage and turnips. We very seldom got our red cross packages as we were suppose too. But it is surprising how you can stretch things and make out without being too hungry. We were each given a bowl, a spoon, knife and fork and two pitchers for coffee and a two gallon bucket to cook in.

A person should see what the boys managed to make with tin cans and pieces of wire some of our boys made dippers and a potato masher. They made baking pans and we even made meat loaf with bread crumbs and meat. Also puddings with bread crumbs and raisins and prunes.

Sometimes for breakfast we had bread cereal. Then sandwiches and coffee for dinner and potatoes, meat and baby cabbage or turnips

29. For supper. We didn't have a lot to eat but we managed to get by ok. After being here a week our ball gunner joined us. He had recovered from blood poisoning ok.

I was assigned to keep the hall and toilet of our building as my job. This was an easy job and gave me something to do to keep from going nuts.

We have a roll call here twice a day and quite often a surprise roll call in our rooms at night. When we first arrived there were about six thousand officer P.O.W. they have been coming in at the rate of about two hundred a week. They are all flying officers and are all good fellows.

30. There have been thousands of attempts to escape but only one man had made it in over six years. There is bobbed wire all around and towers with machine guns and search lights about every 100 ft.

Kearns our pilot went to the hospital upon arrival here with diphtheria. He stayed there a month but came out looking fine.

Life in a P.O.W camp is pretty dull. We were given four decks of cards and someone is always playing cards of some kind. We have heard the same stories a hundred times. We don't complain though; we are too thankful to be alive. I am sure our biggest worries are of our families and loved ones at home. We worry about whether they know if we are alive or not. We know of course they will worry.

31. We are allowed to write two letters and four post cards a month, but we don't know if they go through or not. We have learned from the older fellows that we will be here about seven months

before we get any mail.

From the time we reached here it has been getting colder and colder. It gets around 50 degrees below zero here in Feb. We are only about four miles from the Baltic Sea. Nothing in sight but snow and ice. We can only use the inside toilet from nine P.M. until eight A.M. we have to walk about a block to wash and shave and the wind will freeze water on your hands and face if you don't dry carefully. A mystery to me is why in the world the water in the

32. Pipes in the outside toilets doesn't freeze and break the pipes. We are allowed to keep our lights on until ten P.M.

Then comes the tough part for me. Every night I lie for hours thinking of Anne. If she is well and worrying about me. How dad is getting along. Thinking of all the things we used to do in civilian life. Most of all I think about being able to go home when this mess is all over.

I am hoping this will be over some time in Feb or March. It may take months for us to get home and we may get home in just a few weeks. Any way or time it does happen it will all be worth all of this to be

33. Back with Anne again. I don't think I will want too much out of life when I get home. Most of all I want to be with Anne again. Then I want my friends and a decent place to live.

I want a good bed with pillows and never have to go to bed hungry and cold again. This I think will be all I really need. I have been cold before for an hour or so but I never knew what it could be like to be cold for over 30 days.

I had been hungry I thought but a person would have to go for a month like we did to really know how terrible it can be. I know I have read before about people being hungry but

34. Now I know I never realized how it really felt.

There won't be much more to this story if you can call it that. Nothing much happens here exciting. Every once in a while the

Germans pull a surprise search and if they ever find this I will be put in solitaire on bread and water but I want to get this written down. With nothing to do your mind is bound to get dull and I don't trust mine very far, especially on dates. Of course lots of this I will never forget and will wish that I could. This part I am writing on the 25th of Jan.

Have had this hidden for some time. Have had several searches but so far this hasn't been found. The fellows made a cake and gave me a big surprise for my birthday. They used pipe cleaners and wrote happy birthday. Also on my birthday I started work as a cook.

35. In a new mess hall. We only cook German rations, such as potatoes and horse meat cabbage and turnips and heat water for coffee twice a day. This helps pass the time a lot.

We have had some bad weather, several blizzards with around 40 degrees below zero. I made a calendar back in November but it only goes as far as the end of February. I still hope I won't have to add any more months. Our lights and water were off several days ago. We had to melt snow to get any water at all

36. This is being written on the 3rd day of February We are still eating fair. We are getting nearly a package a man per week with a few potatoes and cabbage once in a while. We haven't had any new men arrive lately. We hope it is because Germany is getting hard pressed for transportation. I am still hoping for an end to all of this sometime this month. I may be off by months but that is all we can do is hope.

We were told yesterday that we can't write or receive any more mail

37. This also makes us feel that things are really getting tough for the Germans As for me I wish that Germany would surrender. I have been in the air and also on the ground and I know how horrible war can be. It is terrible that so many people have to be slaughtered, even though they are your enemies. Sure wish I could hear

from Anne. I keep dreaming of home, I can only hope she is well. Almost time for lights out so must stop for this time.

4 |

TREASURED LETTER

In addition to his diary and poems, Marvin kept this letter from General George C. Marshall. This was mailed to those who served in the Army, and these words inspired Marvin for the rest of his life.

General of the Armies

MESSAGE FROM THE CHIEF OF STAFF

You are being discharged from the Army today — from your Army. It is your Army because your skill and your patriotism, your labor and courage and devotion have been some of the factors which make it great. You have been a member of the finest military team in history. You have accomplished miracles in battle and supply. Your country is proud of you and you have every right to be proud of yourselves.

You have seen, in the lands where you worked and fought and where many of your comrades died, what happens when the people of a nation lost interest in their government. You have seen what happens when they follow false leaders. You have seen what happens when a nation accepts hate and intolerance.

We all are determined that what happened in Europe and in Asia must not happen to our country. Back in civilian life you will find that your generation will be called upon to guide our country's destiny. Opportunity for leadership is yours. The responsibility is yours. The nation which depended on your courage and stamina to protect it from its enemies now expects you as individuals to claim your right of leadership, a right which you earned honorably and which is well deserved.

Start being a leader as soon as you put on your civilian clothes. If you see intolerance and hate, speak out against them. Make your individual voices heard, not for selfish things but for honor and decency among men, for the rights of all people.

Remember, too that NO American can afford to be disinterested in any part of his government, whether it is county, city, state or nation.

Choose your leaders wisely — that is the way to keep ours the country for which you fought. Make sure that those leaders are determined to maintain peace throughout the world. You know what war is. You know that we must not have another. As individuals you can prevent it if you give to the task which lies ahead the same spirit which you displayed in uniform.

Accept that trust and the challenge which it carries. I know that the people of America are counting on you. I know that you will not let them down.

Goodbye to each and every one of you and to each and every one of you , good luck!

/s/ George C. Marshall

/t/ GEORGE C. MARSHALL

General of the Armies, Chief of Staff

MESSAGE FROM THE CHIEF OF STAFF

    You are being discharged from the Army today -- from your Army.
It is your Army because your skill and your patriotism, your labor
and courage and devotion have been some of the factors which make it
great. You have been a member of the finest military team in history.
You have accomplished miracles in battle and supply. Your country is
proud of you and you have every right to be proud of yourselves.

    You have seen, in the lands where you worked and fought and where
many of your comrades died, what happens when the people of a nation
lost interest in their government. You have seen what happens when
they follow false leaders. You have seen what happens when a nation
accepts hate and intolerance.

    We all are determined that what happened in Europe and in Asia must
not happen to our country. Back in civilian life you will find that
your generation will be called upon to guide our country's destiny.
Opportunity for leadership is yours. The responsibility is yours. The
nation which depended on your courage and stamina to protect it from its
enemies now expects you as individuals to claim your right of leadership,
a right which you earned honorably and which is well deserved.

    Start being a leader as soon as you put on your civilian clothes.
If you see intolerance and hate, speak out against them. Make your individual voices heard, not for selfish things, but for honor and decency
among men, for the rights of all people.

    Remember, too, that No American can afford to be disinterested in
any part of his government, whether it is county, city, state or nation.

    Choose your leaders wisely -- that is the way to keep ours the
country for which you fought. Make sure that those leaders are determined
to maintain peace throughout the world. You know what war is. You know
that we must not have another. As individuals you can prevent it if you
give to the task which lies ahead the same spirit which you displayed in
uniform.

    Accept that trust and the challenge which it carries. I know that
the people of America are counting on you. I know that you will not let
them down.

    Goodbye to each and every one of you and to each and every one of
you, good luck!

                        /s/ George C. Marshall
                        /t/ GEORGE C. MARSHALL
                           General of the Armies,
                              Chief of Staff

5 |

MY DARLING IS WAITING
FOR ME

About two months after Marvin was shot down, he was finally able to send a telegram to Anne from the prison camp with the help of the Red Cross. He assured her he was okay and comfortable. These telegrams were monitored by the Germans, and you can see what he publicly writes to comfort Anne is much different than the conditions he describes in his secret diary.

Marvin tells her he realizes their Christmas apart was horrible, but he's able to survive what he's going through knowing that she's waiting for him.

Western Union 1945 Feb 2 AM 8:07

Mrs Anne E Doyle = 1506 North Veitch Street Arlington, VA

"Anne Darling, We received good treatment and are pretty comfortable. Don't worry about me. Am safe and well. Reached my permanent camp —address Stalag Luft 1. Refer to Red Cross regarding full address, letters, packages, etc. notify dad, write often. I know we both had a bad Christmas darling, but I can stand it as long as I know my darling is waiting for me. Just thank God I'm alive and the Red Cross. Pray for an early end of the war. Will write soon. Loving you, missing you, I love you my darling. Lovingly, Marvin

CPL Marvin W Doyle 33636258"

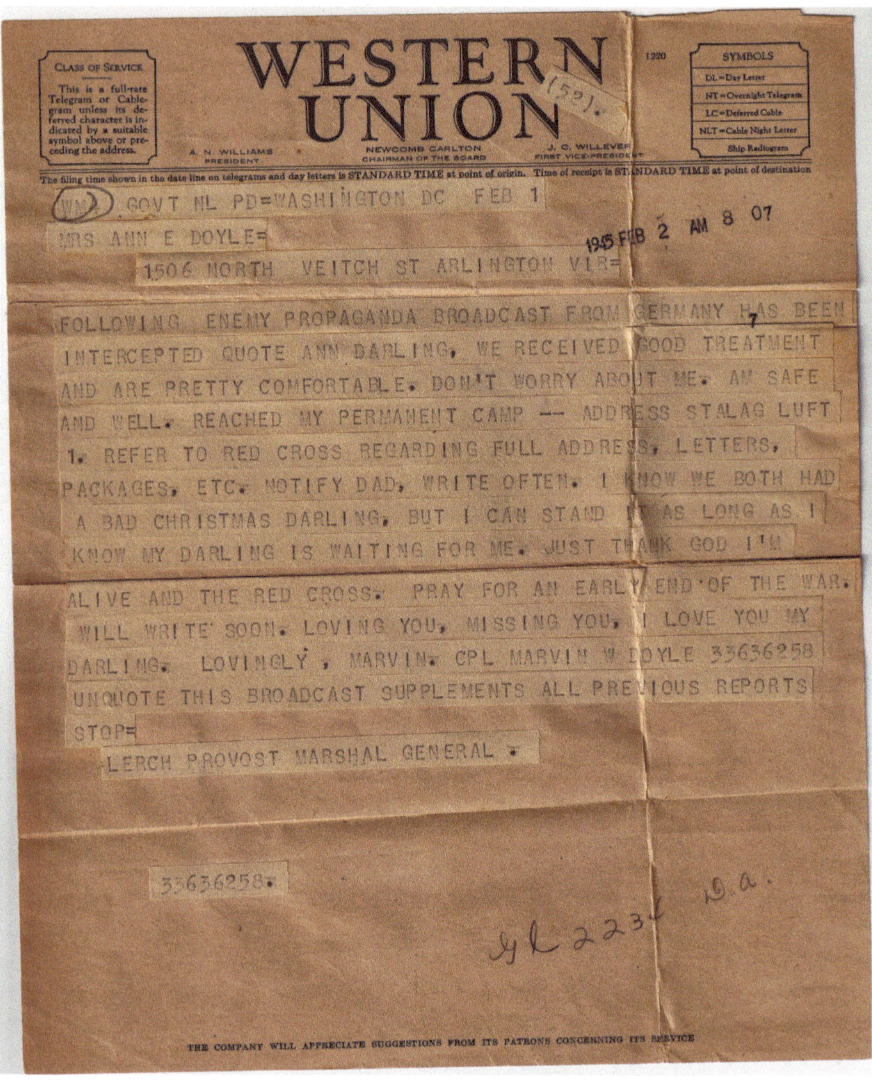

6

POEMS BY MARVIN DOYLE

The Red Cross parcels that arrived at the prison camp with food and toiletries also included notebooks. Soldiers were encouraged to keep busy by writing things down such as poems, recipes or drawings. The Nazi captors monitored what was written in these notebooks and would confiscate them and punish the airmen if anything suspicious was written.

So, Marvin kept his personal diary hidden, but he did write and draw in two Red Cross notebooks. He wrote the names and addresses of other POWs with plans of keeping in contact with them after the war. He also wrote several poems while being held captive.

Here are his poems.

MICHELLE WRIGHT

"Our Kreige Land Home."

...nd home is a helluva place
...around a very small space

Stalag Luft 1 Barth Ger.
Sgt. Marvin W. Doyle
A.S.N. 33636258 - Kreige-6694
Kriegsgef. hilfe
Aide Prisoners de Guerre
War Prisoners Aid   Y.M.C.A.

Stalag Luft 1
Sgt. Marvin W. Doyle
A.S.N. 33636258 - Kreige-6694
Y.M.C.A.

"An escort of P-...
...! Hedy Lamarr is a be...
Madeline Carroll is...
...t you'll find if you qu...
Among any bombe...
...or the lovliest thing...

"A P.O.W.'s Lament."

...Listen and I'll tell you a story,
Of something that happened to me.
...o profit by my experience,
And dont cross over the sea.

I was doing fine and dandy,
With three good meals a day.
But now I'm in a prison camp
Starving my year away.

"Toast to a Gunner"

Here's to the all of us,
The big and small of us.
Foolish or wise, whichever
We are.

Here's to the dead of us,
All those gone ahead of us.
Picking their way on a planet
Or a star.

Laugh while life is left in us,
The morning may finish us.
As death makes no choice of the wise
or the dunce.

Why should it worry us,
If death should hurry us.
All of the living must die
But once.

Courage

It's easy to be nice boys, when everything is okay.
It's easy to be cheerful, when things all go your way.
But can you hold your head up and take it on the chin.
When your heart is breaking and you feel you must give in.

It was easy back in Italy, among all the friendly folks.
But now you miss your comrades voice, their joyous songs and jokes.
The road ahead is stony, and if you're not strong in mind.
You'll find it isn't long before, you're lagging far behind.

You've got to climb the hill boys, no use turning back.
There's only one way home and it's not along their tracks.
So remember you're Americans, and when you reach the crest.
You'll see a valley cool and green, America at her best.

You know that there is a saying, sunshine always follows the rain.
And soon you'll come to realize, that joy will follow pain.
Let courage be your password, fortitude be your guide.
And when you feel you must complain, remember those who died.

Toast to a Gunner

Here's to the all of us,
The big and small of us.
Foolish or wise, whichever
We are.

Here's to the dead of us,
All those gone ahead of us.
Picking their way on a planet
Or a star.

Laugh while life is left in us,
The morning may finish us,
As death makes no choice of the wise
Or the dunce.

Why would it worry us,
If death should hurry us.
All of the living must die
But once.

Our Kriege Land Home

Author's Note: "Kriegies," short for Kriegsgefangener (German for POW).

Our Kriegeland home is a helluva place
With barbed wire around a very small space
We spend our time from morning till night
Just loafing around and cussing our plight.

We practically live out of a bowl and a cup
And duck our tools, when there's an "enemy up."
We all have our troubles, and get mad to the core
At being crossed up by engines, numbers 2, 3, and 4.

We talk of the good things, we left behind
And all that's nice, we expect again to find
When our spirits are high, or when they're low
We console ourselves with "Come on Joe."

I Never Had It So Good

I do nothing all day long
But lie here on my back
I draw full pay, I'm not charged
For food or rent or sack

My meals when it's time to eat
Are served here in my room
I have but to rest and wait
Until the day of doom

I have a dozen bell boys
Outside on call for me
But each one carries a gun
Protecting me you see

It's not everywhere these days
Along with the war and all
That you can get full light and heat.
And an individual stall.

Yet with all that I have said
I want it plainly understood
That I'm just kidding when I say
I've never had it so good.

Captured Airmen

We are the men who no longer fly
Amid the trends of fighters and flak.
We are the ones who are forced to stand by.
To the fight, we will never go back.

Our small domain is encircled by wire.
Not even the ground can we roam.
But must patiently wait, the war does require.
Please God, why can't we go home.

On days when the weather is clear
And we gaze up into the sky.
Sometimes we can see what our captors fear
Our own planes flying by.

Then we on the ground see the scorching flak
And we send up an ardent prayer.
To ask him to guide them safely back
Our classmates of the air.

They are brave boys we flew with.
Some of them have yet to die.
Others will come to join us here.
While the rest continue to fly.

Some day when the war is over
And we hear of the battles won.
Let's hope that he will have a record
Of the glorious deeds they have done.

A.T.C. Boys

*Author's Note: Air Transport Command (A.T.C.) was the strategic
airlift component of the United States Army Air Force during WWII.*

Mom, take down your service flag,
For your son is in the A.T.C.
He's S.O.L. but what the hell,
He's safe as safe can be.
He's flown all over England
And half way up the Nile.
But I'll be damned if he's ever flown
Even a part of a combat mile.

Liberator Song

Oh! Why did I join the Air Corp?
Mother, dear mother knew best.
I'm lying beneath the wreckage.
A "Lib" all over my chest.

The "Lib" is a very good airplane,
Constructed of rivets and tin.
With a top speed of over a hundred,
The only ship with the headwind built in.

If you ever lose an engine,
And you don't know which way to turn.
Just reach up on the instrument panel,
And push the button marked crash, spin, or burn.

If you ever run into ack-ack;
Or an "ME" makes a good pass.
Grab your chute and start moving,
To hell with the ship, save your ass.

As Flak Goes By

To the tune of "As Time Goes By," the song made famous in the 1942 film Casablanca.

You must remember this,
That flak don't always miss.
And one of you may die,
The fundamental things apply
As flak goes by.

And when the fighters come,
You hope you're not the one.
To tumble from the sky,
The odds are always high
As flak goes by.

It's still the same old story,
A tale of too much gory.
Some brave men have to die,
The odds are too damn high.
As flak goes by.

Solitaire

And so another day goes by,
On the wall another mark.
Twilight fades from the sky,
My lonely cell grows dark.
A pale moon makes the evening known,
The hushed birds seek their nest
And my thoughts are turning home,
To the ones I love the best.
Thus I mark another day,
In the gloom I bow my head
And pray for my love ones far away,
Then turn to my prison bed.

Axiom

You can always tell a gunner -
By his hands and vacant stare.
You can always tell a bombardier -
By his manner debonair.
You can always tell a navigator -
By his pencils, books and such.
You can always tell a pilot -
But you cannot tell him much.

Death of a B-24

She lay there, burning and battered
A queen who died in flight,
Her wings were severed from her
No more would she revel in flight.

No more would she thrill to her power
To the roar of the engines she knew,
No more would she hear the gay chatter
Of the carefree men of her crew.

No more would the staccato music
Of her guns forever on guard,
Thrill her in stirring battle
They lay now useless and charred.

I watched the embers last glowing
The smoke that rose in a wave,
The wind would scatter her ashes
And erase the mark of her grave.

They say the fall of a sparrow
Is recorded in the heavenly court,
So surely the judges in heaven
Log the death of a brave flying fort.

A Kriege's Resolve

Author's Note: "Kriege" is short for Kriegsgefangener (German for POW), and Jerry/Jerries is a nickname for Germans).

I think that I shall never see,
A meal that will not appeal to me.
I'll admit that in days gone by,
I've often left a small piece of pie.
Or maybe even a small piece of meat,
I've left on my plate and didn't eat.
But now it is my first resolve,
To quickly make all food dissolve.
Should any dumb unknowing fool,
Leave around to make my mouth drool.
And I'm sure that I won't hesitate,
To take the last small piece of cake.
Meals aren't missed by fools like me,
I know I'd even molest a harmless pea.

A Gunner's Day

A gunner's day is never done.
Up at dawn, before the sun.
With the roar of engines in his head.
Wishing he could have stayed in bed.

Chow at four, fried eggs and such.
He won't have time to eat too much.
Briefing at five, the crew is there.
As always, anxious, to be in the air.

See to your chute, ammo your gun.
For the boys all know it's not for fun.
Jerry will be there, high in the blue.
Waiting for someone, perhaps for you.

Take-off at six, or maybe six-thirty.
Hope no one has a gun, that is very dirty.
Form with the group, at 12,000 feet.
See that formation, it really looks neat.

Put on your mask, for the air is thin.
Off to the battle, some with a grin.
We're over water, now test your gun.
The enemy coast, now comes the fun.

Flak at six, and flak at twelve.
Lookout boys the bombardier yells.
"Here come the fighters, coming in low.
Maybe ours, don't shoot till you know"

They are P-51s and P-38s.
Our escorts are here, they're never late.
They're fighting fools each man and his ship.
There isn't a ship, they couldn't lick.

The air is cold, just fifty below.
Turn up the heat, don't freeze your toe.
A sharp lookout, for the target is near.
We don't care to meet the enemy here.

Target below, there is plenty of flak.
Bombs away boys, we're heading back.
Coming out of the sun, there's an enemy ship.
Aim true boys, we still have more trips.

There goes one down, another one too.
Our fighters are busy to see none get through.
There's flame in the sky and another goes down.
The pilot bails out makes it safe to the ground.

They are on our tail, our guns start to roar.
There's blood on your gun, but you shoot as before.
Your ship is hit but it stays in the air.
You think of your loved ones, and say a prayer.

Smoke from the target, leaps high in the sky.
We'll show those Jerries, we know how to fly.
Our fighters have left us, of those that are left.
Our fighters got some, we got the rest.

We've been up six hours, two more to go.
Though we are doing 200, it seems very slow.
Italy at last, of this we're informed.
To think of our buddies, who will not return.

Wheels hit the ground, with a screech and a bump.
Our ship brought us back, over the hump.
We are over the field, the crew gives a sigh.
we've finished another, to do or to die.

We're tired and dirty, thirsty and sore.
It isn't a picnic, this thing called war.
First clean your guns and do it well boys,
For that gun is life, his, mine and yours.

A sandwich and coffee, your chute to turn in.
Then down to the briefing room, turn in your gun.
Two meals a day, some in the night.
Gets on your nerves, but we're ready to fight.

The mess hall is warm, in the cold of the night.
You sit down to eat, and talk between bites.
You talk about fighters, ours and theirs too.
And of the fellows, who didn't get through.

Of ship going down, exploding in the air.
The bullets that missed, your head by a hair.
Your ships full of holes, guess Bob's pretty bad.
He has a flak fragment, lodged in his head.

Then head for the sack, around ten - fifteen.
A letter from home, another from Gene.
We're for you they wrote, then you know you've won.
For a gunner's day is never done.

"END"

A Mission Today

There's a mission today, and you're scheduled to fly.
So wait by the ship, and look at the sky.
It's cloudy up there, and the wind starts to blow.
But the mission's not scrubbed, "get in and go."

Your nerves are on edge, you cuss and you swear.
If this damn ship flies, you'll lose your bet.
But the ship takes off, as you settle down low.
And cast a longing glance, at the ground below.

Well the ship will fly, while the engines run.
So you take your post, at your trusty gun.
And you check to see, if it's working right.
That the round's not short, nor the headspace tight.

Now check your chute, and try your phone.
It doesn't work, and you heave a groan.
You struggle and test, with the blasted thing.
And it's finally fixed, for you hear it sing.

You call the pilot, and tell him you're set.
And the radio man, breaks in on the net.
And the rest of the crew, all check in turn.
Except in the nose, they'll never learn.

You've joined the squadron, you've joined the group.
And the vapor tails, are as thick as soup.
Your breath comes short so you check your hose.
And you cuss like hell, cause the damn thing's froze.

You clear the ice, so you can breathe again.
It's the life for birds, but not for men.
Your face is cold, and your mask's too tight.
So you pull it off, and fix it right.

You're climbing fast so you look behind.
To see if the squadron is still in line.
The formation looks good, and is staying tight.
So you figure everything is going right.

The hours pass slow, until you are there.
Your eyes smart and burn, from the glare.
Of a sun that's cold, as a chunk of ice.
For the temperature is very, very far from nice.

You've never seen it, so damnable cold.
It tightens up, with a savage hold.
Your fingers freeze, to the grips of your gun.
And you wonder who said, that flying is fun.

But you sweat it out, and stay at your post.
If you leave you know the reports read "lost".
If heaven's this cold, you'll choose to dwell.
In the hottest furnace, they've got in hell.

The pilot calls, you're getting close.
Recheck your guns, and oxygen hose.
You pull your helmet, and flak suit tight.
And pray to God, that all goes right.

The navigator calls, you're on the "I.P."
But your eyelids are froze, and you cannot see.
So you pull out the ice, from the frozen lash.
And you see a fighter, coming in like a flash.

You grab your gun, and fire a burst.
The bastard goes down, but he's started a thirst.
That burns your throat and your mouth goes dry.
As you spot another, way off in the sky.

You line him up, in the ring of your sight.
And you get all set, for a damn good fight.
Now, he is coming in, and doesn't stop.
Until you hear your upper, start to pop.

Then there's a puff and a burst of flame.
And you add a fighter to the gunner's claim.
Now you're rid of two, but you call in more.
You cuss and pray, that their aim is poor.

It makes you mad, and you feel mean.
As you think of home, and places you've seen.
It's just a thought and it passes fast.
And you fire like hell, as a Jerry dives past.

You'll never know, if you knocked him down.
No time to watch him keep looking around.
They're swarming now, like angry bees.
A "twenty" comes through, and you feel the breeze.

They make their attacks, in a steady pass.
And you're willing to bet, they got your ass.
But you track them in, and get their range.
You're enjoying yourself, though that sounds strange.

It's fifty below, but you're wringing wet.
And your foreheads covered with frozen sweat.
With a final pass the Jerries drop back.
And you know damn well, you're headed for flak.

It's coming up now, and bursting fast.
It's coming so close you can feel its blast.
So you make yourself small and try to pray.
And you hope that this, is your lucky day.

Your bombardier calls, "You are on the run."
And you wait to hear, the job is done.
The "bombs away," comes over the wire.
But you are watching a ship, go down on fire.

The stuff is still bursting and black.
And you cuss the bastard who invented flak.
It pounds on the ship like the angry surf.
You're scared as hell, but you keep your nerve.

Your skipper is wise, and he's doing his stuff.
Back there in the tail, the ride is rough.
The ship is hit, cause you feel the jolt.
Your guns swing free, as you lose your holt.

You feel her lurch, and start to drop.
And over the phone comes "feather that prop."
Then smoke streams back from number two.
But your pilot's quick, and pulls her through.

Now she's under control, and flying level.
That skipper of yours is a cool headed devil.
You're out of the flak and the ship still flies.
And you look behind at the smoky skies.

The group behind is in the flak now.
And is catching hell from stern to bow.
You watch two ships, that go falling down.
They both blow up when they hit the ground.

But you're feeling good, cause you've got your hide.
You've beat the flak but what a ride.
There's still three engines running good.
You're headed for home, thinking of food.

The pilot calls, at twelve thousand feet.
"Pull off your mask, and turn down the heat."
You strike a match and light a fag.
And inhale deep that first swell drag.

Soon you're over the field and circling around.
Next into the pattern then back on the ground.
Then you taxi up to your parking space.
You've made it again with the good Lord's grace.

Clear your guns and raise the cover.
Then scramble out and look her over.
The ground crew's there with a silly grin.
To ask you, "where the hell have you been?"

She's full of holes, from her nose to her tail.
But she went and came and didn't fail.
Just above where your head had been.
You could drive a truck, through the vertical fin.

But it's time to brief, so you grab the truck.
And you realize too, that you've had good luck.
Talk the mission over, on the trip to the group.
Where S-2 briefs and gets all the poop.

Your job is done so down to the tent.
Then head for chow like a man hell bent.
Those empty seats, kind of spoil the meal.
You've lost some pals, but it doesn't seem real.

You wait awhile and watch the door.
But they don't come back like they did before.
Go try to forget it, and think of tomorrow.
You've paid the right but not the sorrow.

It's cloudy tonight, sort of looks like rain.
But the bulletin board reads "OP's" again.
The target tomorrow? It's hard to say.
Sweat it out again, in the usual way.

This story goes on, it has no end.
You lose a ship and you lose a friend.
Maybe the day will come when you won't come back.
And they'll chalk you up to fighters and flak.

It's a helluva life and you feel the strain.
But you'll do the whole thing all over again.
Still you pray for the day when there'll be no war.
So you can see what the hell you're fighting for.

You are doing your job we're winning the fight.
You're doing your best to make things right.
Just hope that you'll live and someday see.
A lasting peace, in a world that is free.

"END"

An Escort of P-38s

Oh! Hedy Lamar is a beautiful gal,
Madeline Carroll is too.
But you'll find if you query a different theory,
Among any bomber crew.

For the loveliest thing of which one could sing,
This side of the heavenly gate,
Is no blonde or brunette of the Hollywood set,
but an escort of P-38s.

In the days that have passed, with tables massed,
with glasses of scotch and champagne.
It's quite true that sight is a thing of delight
To us intent on feeling no pain.

But no longer the same, nowadays in this game,
As we recall this and that.
Take your sparkling wine, everything fine, make mine
an escort of P-38s.

Byron Shelly and Keats, ran a dozen dead heats,
describing views from the hills.
Of valleys in May when winds gently sway,
An army of bright daffodils.

Take your daffodils Byron, the wild flowers Shelly,
yours is the myrtle friend Keats.
Just reserve me those cuties flying American beauties,
An escort of P-38s.

Sure we're braver than hell on the ground all is well,
In the air it's a much different story.
As we sweat out our track, thru fighters and flak,
We're willing to share all the glory.

Well they wouldn't reject us, so heaven protect us,
and when all this shooting abates.
Give us the courage to fight them and one more item,
an escort of P-38s.

"END"

A POW's Lament

Now listen and I'll tell you a story,
  Of something that happened to me.
So profit by my experience,
  And don't cross over the sea.

I was doing fine and dandy,
  With three good meals a day.
But now I'm in a prison camp,
  Starving my rear away.

I had no cares or worries,
  My mind was always at ease.
Until some smart sergeant told me,
  I was going to fly in the breeze.

They shoved me in a "B-24,"
  And flew me right across.
They told me that I had no say,
  "Uncle Sam" was still the boss.

But when I got to Italy,
  And saw the fix I was in.
I knew the lie they had told me,
  Surely must have been a sin.

Every thing went very well,
  For the first few months.
Then they told me that I was flying,
  Right over old Berlin.

The fighters they came in droves,
  Just as our bomb load fell.
And things began to happen,
  When the pilot rang the bell.

Now I thought that I'd be very smart,
  And walk back right thru France.
And capture the whole German army,
  Without even giving them a chance.

But I found that I wasn't so very good,
  When it came to trapping the hun.
For all they needed to capture me,
  Was one small boy, and a gun.

So they put me in a box car,
  And shipped me off to camp.
I asked them for food and water,
  But they kicked me, and called me a tramp.

Now I'm behind four high fences,
  Eating stew once a day.
And it's looking very probably,
  For the duration, here's where I'll stay.

But I guess that it is all for the best,
  And will turn out good in the end.
And Germany will soon find out,
  What is inside American men.

For when this war is over,
  We will march thru old Berlin.
And the Fuhrer will be singing,
  "The Yanks have done it again."

7

THE UNDERGROUND NEWSPAPER

When Marvin arrived at the prison camp he was put into the North 3 Compound, block 306, room 13. The Germans had just constructed it two weeks before Marvin's arrival as part of the camp expansion. It was the worst of all the barracks with barely any heat, inadequate toilets, and no kitchen. Marvin was assigned a bunk bed with a mattress filled with straw.

Stalag Luft 1 sat on a piece of land that jutted up into the Baltic Sea. In the distance to the south Marvin could see a large Lutheran church on the edge of the town of Barth. On the west side of the camp there was a pine forest. Less than a mile away to the east and north lay the Baltic Sea. The camp was in the shape of a backward capital letter L and Marvin's barracks were at the very top of it.

Some men had already been imprisoned here for a couple of

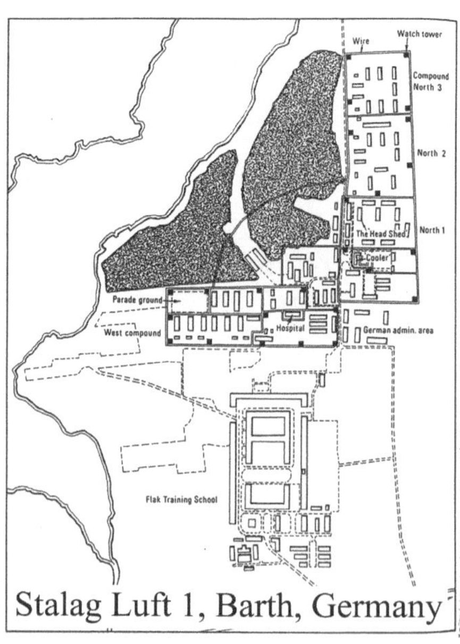

Stalag Luft 1, Barth, Germany

years by the time Marvin arrived. The camp was first erected for Nazi youth and then transitioned into a place to hold British officers before expanding to any Allied airmen. Marvin heard the guards were more relaxed toward the prisoners when the camp first opened. When there was an escape attempt the guards would pick up the escapees and put them in solitary confinement for a few days or perhaps cut their meal rations. But eventually as the war dragged on they were less tolerant. Now, the German guards were impatient. After hundreds of escape attempts the Nazis had had enough. Marvin saw signs posted that said anyone trying to escape could be shot and killed. Morale was at an all-time low.

Marvin would soon learn the camp was divided up into five sections: a West Compound which was also part of the South Compound, North 1, North 2, and North 3 Compounds. These were all fenced off from one another with barbed wire and separated by another section which was the German quarters. At its peak it held about 9,000 airmen from the United States, Great Britain and Canada.

Before Marvin arrived, the gates between the compounds were open during the day but locked at night. But now they were locked all the time. The Germans wanted to to be able to control thousands of prisoners and had them sectioned off. The perimeter was enclosed with a double set of electrified barbed wire with guard towers, machine guns, guard dogs and searchlights.

Marvin joined the roll call which the Germans performed twice a day in which the men were all paraded out in formation and answered when their name was called. The International Red Cross provided items for sports such as ice skates, hockey sticks, soccer balls, softballs, basketballs and board games. There were art supplies for painting and drawing and seeds for a garden. They'd also gotten musical instruments from the YMCA and several orchestras were formed. Some prisoners tried their hand at making moonshine behind the guards' backs. They'd ferment raisins or prunes in sugar. But all of this was not enough to overcome the boredom and depression of being in a prison camp. They were cold, hungry and missed their families. Much of the time was passed by making escape plans.

More than 100 escape tunnels were dug in the time Stalag Luft 1 was operating. Being near the sea, the soil was sandy which made for easy tunneling but the water table was high and that made digging tricky. They could only go down about five feet before getting flooded out. There were other challenges, the barracks were all raised off the ground by almost a foot and that allowed for guard dogs to patrol the trenches under them and search for tunnelers. Sometimes the Nazis would crawl under the barracks to eavesdrop on conversations between the POWs. The airmen nicknamed them "ferrets". The Nazis also installed detectors that would alert them of vibrations if prisoners began working on a tunnel.

Marvin was not about to test the guards with an escape attempt. He tried to keep a low profile because he would do whatever it took to make it out of there alive to get back to Anne. During the day Marvin was allowed to go into two other sections; the North I and West Compounds which contained a kitchen, theater room, church room, library and study room.

But it was back in his own barrack that he would read a secret daily newspaper called POW WOW. It had the latest news updates specifically about the war. The rules of reading it were strict. It was one page, printed on both sides, to be quickly read in small groups, and the last man in the barrack to read it had to destroy it. Its motto was "The only truthful newspaper in Germany - to be read silently, quickly, and in groups of three."

Marvin was amazed at the ingenuity of the underground newspaper that allowed information to flow into the camp. Many servicemen said the daily news updates were the single most important thing that gave them hope. How the paper was recorded, printed and distributed was on a need-to-know basis. Marvin would only later learn how it all was possible. He only knew that getting daily updates kept the servicemen sane. It also let Marvin know his countrymen had not given up. There were still people fighting to free him and to keep the world free.

There are various accounts of how the newspaper came to be and what it became. Through the historic interviews here is the overview of how they made that happen.

The newspaper was called POW WOW which stood for Prisoners of War Waiting on Winning. News came from these main sources:

- German newspapers, magazines, and overheard Nazi conversations translated by POWs who were fluent in German.
- Loudspeakers which broadcast the Nazi war communiques which were mainly propaganda.
- Newly arrived prisoners who brought fresh news and were interviewed upon arrival.
- A secret radio hidden in the south/west compound where the British prisoners listened to broadcasts of the BBC (British Broadcasting Company) and eventually also tuned in to the Voice of America.

It began in 1943 when British Warrant Officer Leslie Hurrell and another officer built a radio receiver and would listen to the nightly BBC broadcast. This was a news source they trusted. The radio was used the first time on February 11, 1942.

They spread the information through the British barracks in a secret bulletin called Red Star. The officers realized the information was important to get to the prisoners. It would give them a sense of hope and prevented them from falling for the Nazi propaganda that was being broadcast on the loudspeakers. The information would be expanded into a daily newspaper.

After building a few different types of radios and hiding them in a few different places, the final one was a two-valve radio receiver hidden in a wall panel behind a bed in the West Compound. There were two fixing nails outside which were disguised on a map mounted on the wall over the bed. The nails acted as terminals to which an aerial wire and earphone cables were attached when in use. They were able to tune-in to the radio stations by using screwdrivers inserted through holes in the wall. If a guard came in for an inspection the wire and screwdrivers could quickly be taken down and the earphones hidden.

The first person to produce the newspaper was American war correspondent Lowell Bennett. He was a 24-year-old journalist with the International News Service. He rode along as an observer on a RAF mission and was shot down over Berlin. He had "civilian" status because he was a reporter and not a soldier. Once imprisoned, he did what he knew how to do; get out factual information to the prisoners. He knew information would be a lifeline for them.

Bennett first began by hand writing the news that reached about a thousand prisoners. The German captors eventually got suspicious how news reports were getting out and put one airman in the cooler for two weeks, trying to get him to divulge the source of information. They warned Bennett they'd take away his civilian status if he was caught as the source of the news. He asked the British officers to get someone else to take over since he was being watched.

In April of 1944, American Colonel Jean R. Byerly brought in American Ray Parker to take over the job of producing POW WOW. Parker had limited experience in reporting but wanted to become a journalist after the war. Before Parker could take over there were several logistics to overcome. Parker was in the North 1 Compound in Barracks 9 which was not near the radio hidden in the West Compound. This would take strategy and nerves of steel.

There was even a greater deal of pressure because American Officer Lt Col. Mackensie who was imprisoned in the camp had just learned the *Voice of America* broadcast included secret messages for POWs in its daily broadcast which aired at 2:00 a.m. Barth, Germany time. Getting the messages would require more than just an overview of the news; this would require a verbatim transcription.

Another challenge was getting power to the radio. The radio ran off the electric power supplied by the camp but power was cut off in the camp at night when the *Voice of America* program aired. The radio would have to be converted to battery power at night and electric during the day.

According to various interviews and writings from those involved, here is how they overcame those challenges and printed an edition of the paper every day until they were liberated. It was discreetly distributed to 9,000 men without fail.

The goal was to listen to three broadcasts a day; two from the BBC and one from *Voice of America (VOA)*. That called for an alarm clock to wake up the operator in time to tune in to the broadcasts. One prisoner had obtained a broken alarm clock. They took it to British Warrant Officer Leslie Hurrell who repaired it and muffled the alarm bell so only the operator would hear it and wake up.

Next, the news had to be quickly written down from the BBC and written out verbatim from the *VOA*. They recruited an American proficient in shorthand for this job. Louis V. Trouve from Long Island, New York knew shorthand and was willing but there was a problem; he was being held in the South Compound. They managed to somehow move him to the West Compound and right into the barracks where the radio was. Trouve would stay in his bed right beside the hidden radio as he took down the broadcast. If a guard burst in for a surprise inspection he would just pretend to be asleep.

Trouve did this job alone from July 1944 to October of 1944. He was under so much strain they brought in an assistant, Lt. A. Small, RACF to assist him. They would transcribe on stiff toilet paper which was uncomfortable for hygiene but excellent for writing. After the news programs, they'd stay awake and transcribe their shorthand. They would hide their transcription in a tin of dried milk which had a false bottom.

Royal Air Force Warrant Officer Drummond would pick up their transcription every day in the West Compound. Drummond was the liaison between the British officers and American officers and had permission to go between the compounds. He also distributed things like sporting goods and games through the whole camp. While he was subjected to being searched, he could move about with little suspicion. He would put the transcription in his wrist watch which had been hollowed out by removing the inner mechanisms. Before he headed out, he'd set the hands on his watch to the correct time so Germans wouldn't notice his watch didn't tell time. He was able to get through searches with ease. When he got to Barracks 9 of the North 1 Compound he'd read his copy of the BBC and *VOA* news to Parker who would take down the information and Drummond would burn his copy immediately.

The *VOA* transcription was handed over to Lt. Col. Mackensie during the daily morning roll call parade. Mackensie would then decode the secret message left in the broadcast.

Meanwhile, Parker would get busy producing POW WOW for all the prisoners. He'd combine the news reports from *Voice of America*, the BBC, and interviews with new prisoners. Also, the POWs who could speak German would tell Parker about what they heard on German radio or overheard from German guard conversations.

POW WOW was two columns on each side of a legal-size piece of tissue paper. It was printed and duplicated by carbon paper on a typewriter. The camp had one typewriter which was provided to the commanding officer per the Geneva Convention. When they didn't have carbon paper they'd make more by smoking sheets of paper over oil based lamps.

Several copies were made of each edition. One copy was distributed to each barracks in various ways. Sometimes they were hidden in a can of dried milk and tossed over a fence when guards weren't looking. One postal officer J.K. Lash tucked a copy between his teeth and cheek and planned to swallow it if searched.

The paper often had hand drawn cartoons including a series called "Klim Kriegies" which parodied life in the prison camp. The rules for

POW WOW was to destroy it after everyone had read it so there are very few copies that exist.

One day Drummond walked into Barrack 9 with a huge smile on his face. It was June 6, 1944 and Parker was about to hear the breaking news about the success of D-Day. POW WOW broke the news about the invasion of Normandy before American news reports by twenty minutes. And the edition about the fall of Paris beat out American newspapers by two hours. Lowell was cautious about distributing good news too quickly because he didn't want the German soldiers to get suspicious in case the prisoners started cheering.

The Germans always suspected there was a secret radio receiver and continued to search for it but never found it. POW WOW went through the camp every day without fail and gave the Allied prisoners hope.

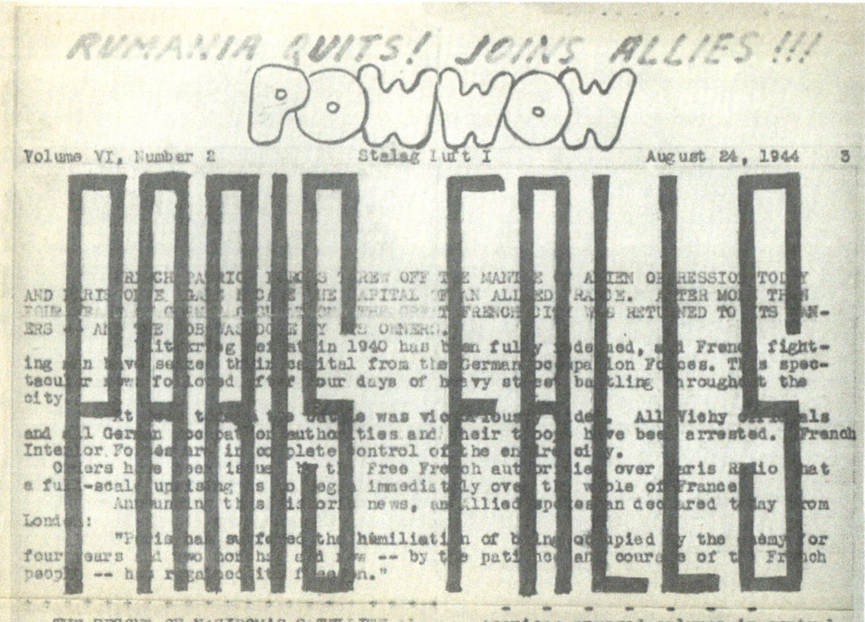

RUMANIA QUITS! JOINS ALLIES !!!

POWWOW

Volume VI, Number 2   Stalag Luft I   August 24, 1944   3

PARIS FALLS

FRENCH PATRIOTS THREW OFF THE MANTLE OF ALIEN OPPRESSION TODAY AND PARIS ONCE MORE BECAME THE CAPITAL OF AN ALLIED FRANCE. AFTER MORE THAN FOUR YEARS OF GERMAN OCCUPATION THE CAPTIVE FRENCH CITY WAS RETURNED TO ITS OWNERS AS AT LAST THE JOB WAS DONE BY THE OWNERS.

The blitzkrieg defeat in 1940 has been fully redeemed, and French fighting men have seized their capital from the German occupation Forces. This spectacular move followed after four days of heavy street battling throughout the city.

At last the Battle was victorious inside. All Vichy officials and all German occupation authorities and their troops have been arrested. French Interior Forces are in complete control of the entire city.

Orders have been issued by the Free French authorities over Paris Radio that a full-scale uprising is to begin immediately over the whole of France.

Announcing this historic news, an Allied spokesman declared today from London:

"Paris has suffered the humiliation of being occupied by the enemy for four years and two months and now -- by the patience and courage of the French people -- has regained its freedom."

THE SECOND OF NAZIDOM'S SATELLITE ALLIES, THE OIL - AND GRAIN - RICH NATION OF RUMANIA, HAS THROWN IN THE TOWEL AND JOINED FORCES WITH THE UNITED NATIONS.

A Royal Proclamation, read over Bucharest Radio early this morning, declared that all of Rumania's resources are to be placed at the disposal of Britain, the United States and Russia -- for use against Germany.

Following the example of Italy, which surrendered little over one year ago, Rumania has officially surrendered to the Allies and Nazi Germany has lost her most important Balkan ally.

Few details were yet available of the dramatic move which closely paralleled the defection of the Kaiser's allies in the final months of the last World War. Most important fact so far to emerge is that Germany's position in the whole of south eastern Europe is now seriously jeopardized.

Her hold on Hungary, Greece and Yugoslavia as well as her political control of Bulgaria are threatened as never before.

Her access to the last remaining oil stocks of Ploesti - frequently bombed by

(continued top col. 2, page 2)

American armored columns in central France kept pace with their French Allies by driving a 40-mile salient eastward from Etamps to the junction of the Seine and Yonne Rivers.

From here, said London, spearheads were advancing on Troyes; 85 miles south east of Paris and less than 150 miles from the German frontier.

The cross-Seine bridgehead was extended 15 miles northward to include the town of Pontoise and was deepened to nearly 15 miles eastward.

West of the river, Allied troops cleared nearly all of Normandy, capturing Lisieux and reaching the area of Louviers, 42 miles to the east and within a few miles of the Seine.

U.S. forces swept around the south of Paris to reach the River Marne, but up to last night no British or American units had yet entered the patriot-held capital.

In the first two and a half months of the Battle for France, announced General Eisenhower's communique, between three and four hundred thousand casualties have been inflicted on the Germans.

Up to the middle of this month, 250,000 casualties were known suffered by

(continued top col. 1, page 2)

THE INVASION OF NORTH-WEST EUROPE HAS BEGUN. Since pre-dawn this morning, Allied shock-troops have been landing on a 95-mile front between Cherbourg and le Havre on the north coast of France. The greatest military operation in history -- the blow to free Europe from Nazism.-- has at last been struck.

A terse statement from the Nazi High Command, at 2pm today, announced:

"The long-expected and long-prepared invasion of the north coast of France started about midnight, after a heavy air bombardment of the coastal defenses.

"Air-borne troops landed at several places between le Havre and Cherbourg, followed by landing craft, supported by light and heavy naval bombardment.

"Our defenses were not surprised. There was bitter fighting in the sectors attacked.

"The air-borne troops were engaged before landing. The paratroops were, for the most part, captured or killed.

"In spite of the fire from enemy naval units, our Channel defenses kept up their fire on the landing craft.

"The action is now in full progress"

= = = = = = = = =

All day yesterday, U.S. bomber and fighter armadas tore at the French coast. London reported that 500 Fortresses and Liberators bombed Boulogne and Calais during the morning.

At noon, very great forces of U.S. and British medium bombers hit specialized objectives all along the coast.

During the afternoon, continuous fighter sweeps were maintained all over the north of France, on dive-bombing and strafing missions.

Last night, in immediate prelude to the landings, R.A.F. Bomber Command struck with all its weight at the coast defenses.

Before dawn, U.S. and British parachutists, glider- and air-borne forces were dropped behind the German coastal

(continued back page)

B-U-L-L-E-T-I-N-S

German Radio, late this afternoon, reported a major naval battle off the coast of Belgium.

Nazi Communique of June 5: "Despite German offer to exclude Rome from the battle area, American armored formations penetrated to the center of the city in the morning of June 4. Bitter street fighting continued until the evening."

Nazi Communique of June 6: "American armored forces were repulsed at Tivoli, fourteen miles north-east of Rome.

North Compound, evening June 6: Our grand-father guardians packed their equipment and drove off in trucks.

8

THE VIOLIN

It is not known if Marvin had any interaction with what has become another famous event to happen at Stalag Luft 1, a violin which was handmade by United States Army 1st Lieutenant Clair Cline from Tacoma, WA. Lt. Cline was imprisoned in Stalag Luft 1 from February 1944 to April 1945. Cline had been locked away in Compound North 1 of room 6, block 6. He was a pilot who'd been shot down in Holland and captured. His wife was also named Anne, and they'd been married for five months before his capture.

To fight boredom, he used his pen knife to carve out models of his B-24 in wood. Lt. Cline was a self-taught violinist who was determined to make a violin to play to lift the spirts of others in the camp. He took bed slats and a chair leg and began to whittle away at the wood to form a violin. Lt. Cline found a sharp piece of glass for carving the instrument's more delicate areas.

He needed some adhesive to hold it all together, and he got the idea of removing any tiny glue balls from chair legs and underneath tables. He ground up the pieces of dried glue and mixed them with water, creating enough glue for the violin. For the violin's curvature, he soaked thin pieces of wood in water and then heated them. Through additional bartering, he secured the sand paper, varnish, pumice and paraffin oil he needed to smooth and protect the wood, as well as to bring out its natural beauty.

The violin's creation became a community project, with both prisoners and guards providing help. Some prisoners scraped glue off the chair rungs, and one of the guards even supplied catgut for the violin's strings. Amazingly, a bow for the violin came from yet another trade. The night of Christmas Eve, a few months after Cline began the violin project he pulled out the finished violin and began to play "Silent Night." The men all sang the Christmas carol together lifting their voices into the holy night.

9

EVACUATION SHOWDOWN

The last notable thing that happened in Marvin's camp is what occurred on the very last day. The liberation didn't go as expected.

Through the POW WOW newspaper, the prisoners began to realize the Allies were getting close to the prison camp. POW WOW reported on April 14th that Patton's Army was advancing from the West and the Russians' Red Army was approaching from the East, just having taken Vienna. Their mood was electric. They started placing bets on which army would arrive first and open the gates to freedom.

Despite the horrific experiences, the Americans wanted to devise a peaceful transfer of power. American Colonel Hubert "Hub" Zemke was the highest-ranking POW at Stalag Luft 1. He was a fighter ace and commanded the 56th Fighter Group known as "Zemke's Wolfpack." He arrived in the camp one week before Marvin. Zemke was there with Marvin in February when the Nazis cut off the Red Cross parcels which had helped to sustain POW food by supplementing the meager German rations. But despite their treatment in the camp, he didn't want revenge; he just wanted peace.

Col. Zemke posted signs around the camp in plain sight for the Germans to encourage a peaceful transfer of power. The goal was to save as many lives as possible when the Allies reached the camp. The signs detailed how the enemy would be treated fairly if they surrendered.

Booming artillery was constantly heard in the distance as the Allies approached. The German guards, of course, knew their time was limited. But they were not ready to give up and allow the prisoners to go free. Nazi Kommandant Oberst von Warnstedt ordered the POWs to begin building sleds for an apparent march to another prison camp.

On April 30 1945, Kommandant Oberst von Warnstedt ordered Colonel Zemke to gather all the airmen and evacuate the entire camp. Colonel Zemke refused to give the order. There was a tense standoff.

The two leaders began to negotiate. Col Zemke held firm. His parents had immigrated from Germany and he was fluent in German which helped in the negotiations. It was finally agreed that to avoid useless bloodshed, the Nazis would go in the middle of the night and head toward the American lines to surrender, leaving the POWs safely behind. The Germans knew the best scenario would be to give themselves up to the United States military rather than the Russians. When the Nazis realized the Russians would make it to the camp first they agreed to leave peacefully and head toward the American troops.

On Tuesday May 1, 1945, the POWs in Stalag Luft 1 woke up to no guards. Just as negotiated, the Germans fled in the middle of the night. The POWs took down the Nazi flag and replaced it with a homemade stars and stripes.

The men got the Nazis' radio and tuned in to the American radio program *Hit Parade*. They were listening for Frank Sinatra's recent version of Cole Porter's song, "Don't Fence Me In." The remake had just hit number one five months earlier, and the airmen joked it should rise to the top of the charts again since their fences were literally coming down. They formed a conga line and danced around the fences singing, "Roll Out the Barrel." While the men celebrated, the senior officers rummaged through their captors' offices and examined all the documents they could find.

The Red Army arrived the next day. Marvin would later talk about the Russians bringing vodka, potatoes and a Russian dance troupe. But they also brought chaos. The American POWs would soon learn that even though the Russians were considered allies in the war, that didn't mean they were friends.

The heavily armed Red Army quickly began to take control of Stalag Luft 1, and Zemke realized he was losing control. The Russians kept the gates locked and refused to let the POWs leave. Reports say it wasn't until almost two weeks later that a U.S. Colonel showed up and threatened to shoot the Soviet Commander if he didn't release the allies. The Russian commander immediately ordered the gates to be opened and the prisoners to be evacuated.

6,000 U. S. Flyers Liberated By Soviets at Camp on Baltic

By the Associated Press.

LUNEBURG, Germany, May 11.—Six thousand American flyers have been liberated by the Russians at Barth, on the Baltic, where the fleeing Germans left their prison camp in charge of the Missoula (Mont.) ace, Col. Hubert C. Zemke.

The flyers at Stalagluft 1 had awaited the arrival of the Russians. Their German guards had fled. Besides the Americans, 300 RAF flyers were liberated.

Col. Zemke was commander of the top-scoring 56th Thunderbolt Group and had been missing since fall, when his fighter plane was destroyed. Two weeks ago a German officer approached him and said:

"We are leaving. The Russians are coming. The camp is in your hands."

Airmen, armed with clubs, were ordered by Col. Zemke to guard the camp, which is directly north of Berlin. Another detachment went to a nearby airfield to dig out mines and prevent the Germans from wrecking it.

Guards were posted around the camp to keep panicked civilians from entering it in their flight from the Russians.

The story was pieced together today by Maj. W. P. Lightfoot, Des Moines, American contact officer for prisoners of war at this clearing center of Luneburg. Maj. Lightfoot questioned 300 American flyers who left Stalagluft 1 and made their way to Luneburg. They were flown from here to Le Havre for embarkation to the British Isles.

These 100 officers and 200 enlisted men left the camp by a "back door," although Col. Zemke was trying to inforce order and have the men remain for evacuation by the Russians, according to a supreme headquarters directive.

The men who sneaked out said they took the chance of getting back to British territory, rather than awaiting evacuation by the Russians through Odessa, a process that probably would take several months.

Some left camp on small boats and crossed 60 miles of open water for Sweden, the escaped men said.

Lt. Col. Frank Eresch, Topeka, Kans., is here waiting permission to go to the camp and help arrange details of the evacuation.

Marvin packed up what few things he had in the camp, but the most precious thing was his secret diary. After 176 days in captivity and multiple searches by the Nazis, he was able to keep his diary hidden and safe. He couldn't wait to let Anne read what he'd been through.

The men marched in groups through the camp and down to the airfield in Barth. They waited on the sides of the runway to climb into the B-17s that would carry them to freedom. The Brits would be flown back to England, and the Americans would go to Camp Lucky Strike in Le Havre, France and wait to get shipped back to the United States.

The evacuation was called "Operation Revival." Crews removed all the armaments out of B-17 bombers to make room for thousands of POWs.

On Sunday, May 13, 1945 Marvin boarded a B-17. It was Mother's Day. Marvin's mother, Adelaide Doyle, had passed away March of 1936 when Marvin was just 25. Marvin was now 34. He would not be able to share with her what he'd been through for the last seven months, but he surely felt her presence that day.

He crowded into the B-17 and flew over the fields of Germany. Looking down, he saw the fields, once erupting with flak, now calm and quiet.

8,944 Happy Vets Landed at N. Y.

NEW YORK, June 3 (N. Y. News).—First in battle, first in victory, 1,453 of the 1st army were the first to come home as a group today—serenaded by a jive-playing Wac band as they steamed into New York harbor.

Three transports, led by the Troopship Monticello, carying the 1st army general staff, filed through the harbor net at noon—to receive a tumultous greeting from thousands lining the shore.

More than 5,200 soldiers, including liberated prisoners and wounded, jammed the Monticello's rails—and gave cheer for cheer as their convoy circled the Statue of Liberty and headed for its berth in Stapleton, S. I.

All told, the convoy brought back 8,944 veterans. The other transports were the Lejeune and the Santa Margarita. After 30-day furloughs, the 1st army general staff, officers and enlisted men will proceed to the Pacific—becoming the first group to make the transfer. It already has the distinction of being the first to land in Europe, first to invade Germany, first to cross the Rhine, first to greet the Russians.

Earlier, before the city was awake, four Liberty ships, including the John B. Hood, debarked nearly 1,500 veterans, mostly liberated prisoners.

The Hood had a gaping hole in its bow and Chief Officer Joseph Sutton disclosed it had been damaged, with 15 other vessels of a 96-ship convoy, in a heavy fog off the Grand Banks last Sunday.

Sutton said two converted transports crashed into icebergs, causing several others to nose together, and menacing 80 helpless tankers, grouped within 150 yards of each other. Sutton said the fog was the densest he had ever encountered.

1st Lt. Irving M. Day, jr., whose wife, Mrs. Marin S. Day, lives at 1 West Everett street, Kensington, Md.

Sergt. Marvin W. Doyle, whose wife, Mrs. Anne E. Doyle, lives at 1506 North Veitch street, Arlington, Va.

1st Lt. Henry R. Lambert, son of Alfred G. Lambert, 2811 Holly street, Alexandria, Va.

2nd Lt. Vivian D. Loving, son of Vivian R. Loving, 1233 North Bluemont drive, Arlington.

S/Sergt. Earl S. Mason, jr., son of E. S. Mason, 409 Cameron street, Alexandria.

Pfc. Isaac H. Moore, whose wife, Mrs. Marguerite M. Moore, lives at 1031 North Nelson street, Arlington.

S/Sergt. Michael E. Udick, brother of Miss Helen J. Udick, Beverly Park Gardens, Alexandria.

Reports on the following men officially listed today as liberated, previously appeared in The Star when next of kin were notified:

2nd Lt. Francis J. Boyle, whose wife, Mrs. Dorothy B. Boyle, lives at 2812 Fifth street N.E.

Capt. Robert P. Cowie, son of Mrs. Mary P. Cowie, 1750 Massachusetts avenue N.W.

1st Lt. William I. Greenough, son of Mrs. Carroll Greenough, 1408 Thirty-first street N.W.

Pfc. Lawrence M. Hill, whose wife, Mrs. Maude E. Hill, lives at 303 Twelfth stret S.E.

T/Sergt. David M. Hovis, brother of Mrs. Calvin W. Spargo, 4019 Kansas avenue N.W.

Pfc. John M. W. Llewellyn, whose wife, Mrs. Mary Llewellyn, lives at 200 Rhode Island avenue N.E.

Capt. Donald L. May, son of Leo C. May, 2208 Wyoming avenue N.W.

Pvt. Edward G. McCarthy, son of Mrs. Margaret E. McCarthy, 3314 Eighth street N.E.

2d Lt. Miles C. McCormack, son of Edward J. McCormack, 2545 Waterside drive.

Pvt. John A. Mountcastle, whose wife, Mrs. Sadie L. Mountcastle, lives at 1342 Emerson street N.E.

Pfc. Robert M. Preston, son of James P. Preston, 5308 Forty-third street N.W.

Capt. Michael J. Quirk, whose wife, Mrs. Mary M. Quirk, lives at 3005 McKinley street N.W.

Pvt. Edward A. Richards, son of Arthur J. Richards, 311 New Jersey avenue S.E.

10

REUNITED

Now that Marvin was a free man, he immediately started making his way back to Anne. After being held captive for 176 days, he had a lot to tell her. He hadn't heard from her and could only hope she waited for him. Marvin arrived in Camp Lucky Strike outside of Le Havre, France along with 8,500 other POWs and immediately sent Anne a telegram. He was limited to fifteen words and he wrote, "Safe. Well. France. Don't. Worry. Write. Dad. Home. Soon. Keep. Loving. And. Waiting. For. Me. "

15 WORD FREE SENDER COMPOSITION PRIORITY MESSAGE

To: MRS ANNE E. DOYLE
(Full name of addressee)

1506 N Veitch St.
(Street and number)

ARLINGTON   VIRGINIA
(City or Town)   (State)

INSTRUCTIONS

One message only to next of kin in US from each Recovered American Military Personnel. PRINT message, including address and signature, in BLOCK LETTERS. Message, exclusive of address and signature, will be 15 words, one word above each of the 15 lines provided below.

SAFE   WELL   FRANCE   Dont   WORRY
WRITE   DAD   HOME   SOON   KEEP
LOVING   AND   WAITING   FOR   ME

SGT. MARVIN W. DOYLE
(Full name of Sender)

DO NOT FOLD THIS FORM

33636258
(Army Serial Number)

With all the confusion of tens of thousands of servicemen trying to get word home, mail was delayed. Anne did not get the message. On June 19th, 1945, the United States Army sent a telegram to Anne that read "The Chief of Staff of the Army directs me to inform you your husband Cpl Doyle Marvin W is being returned to the United States within the near future and will be given an opportunity to communicate with you upon arrival." But once again, the telegram wasn't delivered to Anne.

From France, Marvin took a boat home and didn't land in the New York harbor until June 3rd. Many servicemen described having tears in their eyes as they stood on the deck of the ship, seeing the Statue of Liberty welcoming them home. Marvin immediately made his way to Virginia to get to his dearest Anne.

Anne still wasn't aware he was coming home. Since the war was over and she hadn't heard from him, she didn't know if he'd ever come home to her. When Marvin showed up at their home, Anne was shocked. She was so overcome with emotion, she fainted at seeing his beloved face at her door. It would be a few more days before both telegrams would arrive to say Marvin was coming home.

They were ready to live happily ever after. Marvin showed her his diary and poems. He told her about the unbearable hunger. He told her about the frigid temperatures, so they vowed to start their lives in the warmest place Marvin had ever been, a place he knew from his training days. They moved under the hot sun of Miami. Marvin drove down first and rented an apartment at 1040 NE 78 Road while Anne had to wait a few weeks to officially transfer her job with the telephone company to Miami.

One of the men in Marvin's squadron decided to move to Miami, too. Robert McVay, the radio man and the first man who parachuted out of their plane when it was shot down, also decided to move from Pittsburgh, Pennsylvania. He packed up his things from 1716 Maple Street in Homestead, a borough just outside of Pittsburgh, and started a new life in Miami.

Marvin opened his own gas station and ran the business while basking in the warmth of Florida's bright sunshine with the ocean breeze in his face. But despite the relaxing location, his mind could not fully rest. He was tormented by constant nightmares from his time in the war. Years later, Anne would come to understand Marvin had severe PTSD from his experience. Anne did what she could to reassure him and make him feel safe. Marvin coped the best he could and always told Anne how thankful he was to be back with her. The only thing that would separate them again was his death.

A heart attack took Marvin's life at the young age of 52. It was January 3, 1964. He was buried in Roanoke, Virginia where his parents were interred at Evergreen Cemetery.

Despite being widowed at a young age, Anne never remarried. She moved to Lynchburg, Virginia into the home where her father had lived on Meadow View Drive. She was my next-door neighbor. She never learned to drive and my mother, Gail Wright, would take her to the grocery store every week, to every doctor's appointment, and anywhere else Anne needed to go. Often, Anne would call my mother and ask to ride along on any errands mom was running that day just to get out of the house. Mom and Anne especially enjoyed shopping for antiques to put in my mother's antique shop. As Anne continued to age, my parents cared for her more and more.

Anne passed away peacefully in 2003 at the age of 89 and was buried next to her love, Marvin, in Evergreen Cemetery at the foot of the Blue Ridge Mountains in Roanoke, Virginia.

They are reunited again.

Marvin's
Medals

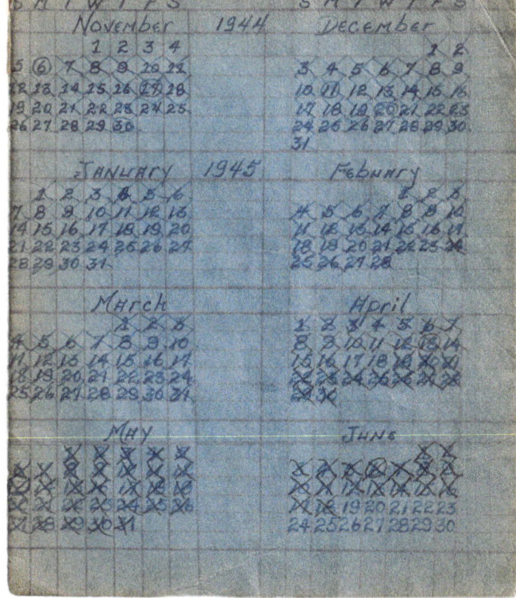

A drawing and calendar from Marvin's notebook.

11

EPILOGUE

Marvin took a big risk documenting his experience and took great care in protecting his diary and poems. He knew the importance of preserving history. Anne kept his things safe for decades and gave them to my mother in hopes of his story being told. After my mother's death, I inherited Marvin's things and wanted to fulfill their wishes. I had no idea what an impact this research would have on me. I spent more than a year organizing, researching and writing *The Secret Diary*. The more I learned, the more I was inspired. Here are the five lessons I learned through the process of writing this book.

INFORMATION IS IMPORTANT

The first lesson is the importance of accurate information. It was so important to the men in Stalag Luft 1, they were willing to risk their lives for it. I can only imagine how those POWs felt when they finally had access to daily news reports from their secret radio and the POW WOW underground newspaper. They knew the Allies were working hard to free them and end the war. They were also able to prepare for what was happening. The U.S. Col. Zemke knew either the Red Army or the U.S. Army would reach Stalag Luft 1 within days. That information helped him negotiate a peaceful release. Without knowing that, he may have had no choice but to go along with the Nazi order to evacuate the camp. Lives were literally saved because of the news reports by the BBC and VOA.

As a broadcast journalist, I have seen the power of verified news in communities. Whether the news is good, tragic, frightening or exciting, I feel the only way people can improve their communities is to know what is happening. Many viewers tell me they don't like to watch the news because it's so often depressing. They ask me how I am able read so much tragic news. I answer that by sharing information, whether exciting, depressing, alarming or even boring, I know that I'm enlightening viewers to things that will help them make better choices to protect their family and improve their neighborhood.

It is also inspiring when we share information about a tragic story and see how our community comes together to help a family in need. The great Fred Rogers from *Mr. Rogers Neighborhood* said when tragedies happen to "look for the helpers." Knowledge empowers people and that is the most rewarding part of my job.

JOURNALING IS IMPORTANT

Another valuable lesson is the power of journaling. The diary is the one thing Marvin protected during his time in the prison camp. He knew the value of having a record to let others know the truth. But he also wrote about the need to relieve his mind from trying to remember the tough details. I found this line in his diary so interesting, "all of the following I am setting down to help remember dates and places only, as most of the happenings I hope I can forget." He seemed to understand how putting things down on paper would relax his mental state.

There is scientific research that shows keeping a daily journal can help us, too. Journaling is an evidence-based strategy to boost mental health and relieve stress. Studies show writing down daily activities or goals can help process thoughts and feelings. It also helps give a feeling of control over chaos. The daily ritual can also help us move past anxieties and improve decision making.

Research has also shown journaling before bed can help you fall asleep faster. This is especially true for anyone who makes a to-do list. It seems once you write down a list, your mind releases it and that allows you to fall asleep faster.

The first time I journaled is when my news director forced me to write a blog for our station's website. Blogs were just getting popular and our website needed some more personal content. Three of us were ordered to participate. The rules on topics were strict: no politics or religion, nothing critical or controversial, and we couldn't promote or complain about a product. In other words, it was destined to be boring. I was frustrated trying to come up with something to post. My brain was forced to find something positive every day. At first it was a challenge and then it was life changing. I had never searched for so many positive things before, and I found there were more wonderful things around me than I could even write about. I began to love it. Searching for positive things and journaling about them certainly changed my outlook on life.

TAKING ACTION IS IMPORTANT

The third lesson from Marvin's story is the importance of taking action. Marvin was inspired by the challenge laid out in a letter by Chief of Staff of the U.S. Army General George Marshall. Marvin kept the letter with his most treasured things. General Marshall was born in Uniontown, Pennsylvania and later attended the Virginia Military Institute. He rose to become Secretary of State and Secretary of Defense.

General Marshall's letter said in part, "You have seen in the lands where you worked and fought and where many of your comrades died, what happens when the people of a nation lost interest in their government."... "If you see intolerance and hate, speak out against them. Make your individual voices heard, not for selfish things but for honor and decency among men, for the rights of all people " .... "remember that no American can afford to be disinterested in any part of his government, whether it is county, city, or nation." Those words are relevant even today.

I am also inspired by how Marvin took action in a life-threatening emergency. As the B-24 was going down in heavy enemy fire, he ran to help his squadron member, Wayne Rinne. Marvin bravely put someone else before himself in that situation. While Marvin was haunted by Rinne's final smile as he jumped out of the plane never to pull his chute, at least he knew he did all he could.

My mother was a great example of this as well. She constantly took action for others. She sacrificed not only for her family but also for Anne Doyle. Anne needed help with groceries and doctor visits and yard work but she also needed friendship. Mom made sure Anne had all those things. Even though Anne needed a lot of help, my mom never complained and would always make sure Anne's needs were taken care of before Anne could even ask for help.

HISTORY IS IMPORTANT

Marvin risked his life to preserve history. He knew if he were caught with a diary he would be punished or even killed, but he thought it was a chance worth taking. He wanted Anne to know the truth about what happened if somehow he didn't survive. But he also wanted the world to know the truth.

Reviewing history also provides a blueprint for the future. It allows us to learn about ourselves and pass those lessons along to future generations. Sometimes our history is something to celebrate and other times it focuses on mistakes we should avoid.

History also provides a lot of precious memories. I've interviewed many homeowners who lost their home to fire and the one thing they wish they'd grabbed as they ran out to safety were photo albums. They have told me everything can be replaced except the pictures. I have come to respect the importance of historical records of both good times and bad times.

GRATITUDE IS IMPORTANT

Marvin wrote about how he had a new appreciation for things he had previously taken for granted: food, warmth, loved ones, and safety. He wrote, "I know I will never be able to make anyone understand how we felt after all we had been through for the past 35 days. Just to be clean and warm and not be hungry. None of us realized how much this meant before."

He went on to say what he was looking forward to when the war was over. "I don't think I will want too much out of life when I get home. Most of all I want to be with Anne again. Then I want my friends and a decent place to live. I want a good bed with pillows and never have to go to bed hungry and cold again. This I think will be all I really need. I have been cold before for an hour or so but I never knew what it could be like to be cold for over 30 days. I had been hungry I thought but a person would have to go for a month like we did to really know how terrible it can be."

In all the research for this book, this is what I will take away the most. I have a new focus to appreciate things that I am blessed with every day. Paying attention to loved ones and not taking them for granted is important. Also, it is important to slow down and realize that even the small things in life deserve my gratitude every single day.

Michelle Wright is an award-winning news anchor for WTAE in Pittsburgh, PA. She has reported live from the scene on the region's biggest news stories including: The Flight 93 crash in Shanksville on 9/11, the Quecreek Mine rescue, and the G-20 Summit. Michelle has also worked as an adjunct professor at three local universities.

Michelle has been honored with three Regional Emmy Awards, a National Headliners Award, an Edward R. Murrow Award, received numerous honors from the Associated Press and the Pennsylvania Association of Broadcasting, honored as a 2010 Woman of Distinction recipient, and a 2011 recipient of the SWPA Media and Mental Health Award.

Michelle began her career at WSET in Lynchburg, Virginia and is a graduate of Liberty University. She is also a beekeeper and sells her honey, Chapel Valley Honey. She renovated a historic chapel called Tarenbee and operates it as a commercial kitchen and event venue.

To have Michelle speak to your organization about The Secret Diary please email her at michellewright@outlook.com.